Praise for

IN THE PRESENCE OF MY ENEMIES

"A powerful story." —*Reader's Digest*

"Remarkably honest and unaffected.
. . . Impressive."
                 —*Publishers Weekly* starred review

"Recommend this awe-inspiring narrative
to a broad audience, who are sure to be
moved by the entire Burnham family's
courage." —*CBA Marketplace*

"The issue . . . is not why an all-powerful
God might choose to subject a man to evil,
but how a man, with God's help, responds
to evil. . . . The Burnhams, under torturous
conditions, befriended their guards, com-
forted their fellow hostages and kept their
faith in a God who seemed to have abandoned them." —*USA Today*

IN THE PRESENCE OF MY ENEMIES

GRACIA BURNHAM

with DEAN MERRILL

God Bless You!

Gracia

TYNDALE
MOMENTUM™

*The nonfiction imprint of
Tyndale House Publishers, Inc.*

Visit Tyndale online at www.tyndale.com.

Visit Tyndale Momentum online at www.tyndalemomentum.com.

TYNDALE, Tyndale Momentum, and Tyndale's quill logo are registered trademarks of Tyndale House Publishers, Inc. The Tyndale Momentum logo is a trademark of Tyndale House Publishers, Inc. Tyndale Momentum is the nonfiction imprint of Tyndale House Publishers, Inc., Carol Stream, Illinois.

In the Presence of My Enemies

Designed by Stephen Vosloo

For information about special discounts for bulk purchases, please contact Tyndale House Publishers at csresponse@tyndale.com, or call 1-800-323-9400.

Library of Congress Cataloging-in-Publication Data

Burnham, Gracia.
   In the presence of my enemies / Gracia Burnham, with Dean Merrill.
      p. cm.
   ISBN 978-0-8423-8138-3 (hc)   ISBN 978-0-8423-8139-0 (sc)   ISBN 978-0-8423-8590-9 (intl)
   ISBN 978-0-8423-8589-3 (Philippine)   ISBN 978-0-8423-8576-3 (NTM)
   1. Burnham, Gracia.   2. Burnham, Martin.   3. Hostages—Philippines—Biography.   4. Abu Sayyaf (Organization)   5. New Tribe Mission—Biography.   6. Missionaries—Philippines—Biography.
7. Missionaries—United States—Biography.   I. Merrill, Dean.   II. Title.
   BV3382.B87 A3 2003
   959.904'092273—dc21   2003002155

Printed in the United States of America

23   22   21   20   19
14   13   12   11   10   9

This book is dedicated to . . . you.
If you prayed for Martin and me
while we were in captivity—
even once—then put your name
here. It is because of your prayers
that I came out alive and am
able to tell the story. Likewise,
I hope to become one
who earnestly prays and cares
for others who are hurting.
We truly need each other,
don't we?

CONTENTS

THE CAPTORS' ROSTER

Of the dozens of Abu Sayyaf who guarded the Burnhams at various times, these were the most prominent. (The title Abu *means "father of." Mang means "uncle.")*

POPULAR NAMES	**"Moktar,"** "Abu Moktar" (see photo section)
OFFICIAL NAME	Khadafi Abubakar Janjalani
ROLE	Leader of the entire Abu Sayyaf (following the 1998 slaying of his older brother, the group's founder); late 20s, but looked younger; quiet; eventually "married" Reina
PRESENCE	Met the hostages upon arrival on Basilan May 31, 2001; left them late September 2001

POPULAR NAMES	**"Musab,"** "Abu Musab" (see photo section)
OFFICIAL NAME	Isnilon Totoni Hapilon
ROLE	Second-in-command of the Abu Sayyaf; knew little English; stern, headstrong; eventually "married" Ediborah
PRESENCE	From the beginning through early May 2002

POPULAR NAMES	**"Omar,"** "Abu Omar"
OFFICIAL NAME	Bakkal Hapilon
ROLE	Brother of Musab; eventually took Sheila for himself but did not formally "marry" her
PRESENCE	Met the hostages upon arrival on Basilan May 31, 2001; stayed through early May 2002

POPULAR NAMES	**"Sabaya,"** "Abu Sabaya" (see photo section)
OFFICIAL NAME	Aldam Tilao
ROLE	Spokesman to the media; negotiator with the government; known for his flair; very good English; eventually "married" Angie
PRESENCE	With the hostages the entire time

POPULAR NAME	**"Solaiman"** (see photo section)
OFFICIAL NAME	Jainal Antel Sali Jr.
ROLE	Prime liaison with the hostages for the first 3 months, due to his education, English fluency; late 30s; former engineer from a wealthy family
PRESENCE	From the beginning through late September 2001
POPULAR NAME	**"Mang Ben"**
ROLE	Early leader of the Burnhams' subgroup; tall, thin, stately appearance; late 30s
PRESENCE	From the beginning until killed in battle early July 2001
POPULAR NAME	**"Hurayra"**
OFFICIAL NAME	Jumadil Arad
ROLE	Friendly toward the Burnhams; mid-20s
PRESENCE	From the beginning through late September 2001
POPULAR NAME	**"Moghira"**
ROLE	Subgroup leader; eventually "married" Fe
PRESENCE	Met the hostages upon arrival on Basilan May 31, 2001; left New Year's Eve 2001
POPULAR NAME	**"Sakaki"**
ROLE	Gracia Burnham's first designated guard
PRESENCE	From the landing on Basilan until he went AWOL July 2001
POPULAR NAMES	**"Bro,"** "Kosovo"
OFFICIAL NAME	Alhamzer Limbong
ROLE	Classic warrior type; big, muscular, well-built, proud of his long, wavy hair; knew just a bit of English but willing to try using it
PRESENCE	From the beginning through late September 2001
POPULAR NAME	**"Zacarias"**
OFFICIAL NAME	Toting Craft Hanno
ROLE	Fun-loving; early 20s; Solaiman's assistant
PRESENCE	One of the original trio to abduct the Burnhams; left due to sickness late September 2001

Other resistance groups operating in the southern Philippines:

- Moro Islamic Liberation Front (MILF)
- Moro National Liberation Front (MNLF)

Moro is an ethnic label for Filipinos who are Muslim. It traces back several centuries to the Spaniards, who used it as a name for a Muslim in their own country. The English translation is "Moor."

THE HOSTAGES' ROSTER

Captured at Dos Palmas Resort on May 27, 2001

MEN

NAME **Martin Burnham**   CAPTIVITY 1 year, 11 days
DESCRIPTION   American missionary pilot from Kansas; age 41; husband of Gracia, father of three
CONCLUSION   Killed by three gunshots June 7, 2002

NAME **Francis**   CAPTIVITY 20 days
DESCRIPTION   Banker; age 50; husband of Tess
CONCLUSION   Released June 15, 2001, after ransom was paid

NAME **Chito**   CAPTIVITY 38 days
DESCRIPTION   Salesman for a cell-phone company; 30s; married, father of three
CONCLUSION   Released July 3, 2001, after ransom was paid

NAME **Reggie**   CAPTIVITY 7 days
DESCRIPTION   Former newspaper executive; VP of a construction company with many government contracts; late 40s
CONCLUSION   Released June 2, 2001, after ransom was paid

NAME **Buddy**   CAPTIVITY 7 days
DESCRIPTION   Publisher of a travel magazine; husband of Divine
CONCLUSION   Abandoned June 2, 2001, after being wounded

NAME **R. J.**   CAPTIVITY 7 days
DESCRIPTION   Buddy and Divine's 8-year-old son
CONCLUSION   Released June 2, 2001

NAME **Guillermo Sobero**   CAPTIVITY 16 days
DESCRIPTION   American contractor from California; age 40
CONCLUSION   Beheaded June 11, 2001

NAME **Sonny Dacquer** CAPTIVITY 6 days

DESCRIPTION Dos Palmas cook

CONCLUSION Left behind, then beheaded June 1, 2001

NAME **Armando Bayona** CAPTIVITY 6 days

DESCRIPTION Dos Palmas security guard

CONCLUSION Left behind, then beheaded June 1, 2001

NAME **Eldren** CAPTIVITY 6 days

DESCRIPTION Dos Palmas security guard

CONCLUSION Left behind June 1, 2001; survived a botched beheading attempt

WOMEN

NAME **Gracia Burnham** CAPTIVITY 1 year, 11 days

DESCRIPTION American missionary from Kansas; early 40s; wife of Martin, mother of three

CONCLUSION Wounded by one gunshot during June 7, 2002, encounter, but evacuated

NAME **Tess** CAPTIVITY 7 days

DESCRIPTION Wife of Francis; a "mother" to Gracia while on the boat; religious and caring

CONCLUSION Released June 2, 2001, in order to arrange ransom for her husband

NAME **Janice** CAPTIVITY 7 days

DESCRIPTION Coworker of Chito; 20s; full of life

CONCLUSION Released June 2, 2001, in order to arrange ransom for Chito

NAME **Rizza** CAPTIVITY 7 days

DESCRIPTION Girlfriend of Reggie

CONCLUSION Released June 2, 2001, after ransom was paid

NAME **Divine** CAPTIVITY 7 days

DESCRIPTION Wife of Buddy, mother of R. J.

CONCLUSION Abandoned June 2, 2001, after being wounded

NAME **Angie** CAPTIVITY 5½ months

DESCRIPTION Sister of Divine; early 30s; single; worked in the family business (travel magazine)

CONCLUSION Ransomed in late August but not released until November 15, 2001

NAME **Letty** CAPTIVITY 7 days

DESCRIPTION Chinese-Filipino businesswoman

CONCLUSION Released June 2, 2001, in order to arrange ransoms for her daughter and niece

NAME **Kim** CAPTIVITY 20 days

DESCRIPTION Daughter of Letty; early teens

CONCLUSION Released June 15, 2001, after ransom was paid

NAME **Lalaine** CAPTIVITY 38 days

DESCRIPTION Niece of Letty; early teens

CONCLUSION Released July 3, 2001, after ransom was paid

NAME **Fe** CAPTIVITY 5½ months

DESCRIPTION Fisherman's daughter from Palawan; age 20; fiancée of Guillermo

CONCLUSION Ransomed in late August but not released until November 15, 2001

Captured at Lamitan hospital on June 2, 2001

NAME **Sheila** CAPTIVITY 5½ months

DESCRIPTION Nurse; married, mother of one son

CONCLUSION Released November 15, 2001

NAME **Reina** CAPTIVITY 4 months

DESCRIPTION Nurse; early 20s; single

CONCLUSION Released in September due to pregnancy

NAME **Ediborah Yap** CAPTIVITY 1 year, 5 days

DESCRIPTION Head nurse; mother of four

CONCLUSION Killed by gunshot June 7, 2002

NAME **Joel**   CAPTIVITY 4½ months
DESCRIPTION   Hospital orderly; early 20s; single
CONCLUSION   Escaped during firefight October 14, 2001

Surnames of surviving Filipino hostages are withheld out of respect for their privacy.

All dates in this chart, and throughout the book, are local time. Central time zone in the United States (e.g., Kansas, Arkansas) is 13 hours behind Philippine time in the summer, 14 hours behind in the winter. (The Philippines, being close to the equator, has no need for a daylight saving time arrangement.)

FOREIGN TERMS

Abu Sayyaf: "father of the swordsman"

Al-Harakatul Islamia: the Islamic movement

alimatok: leeches

"Allah akbar!": "Allah is the greatest!"

apam: Muslim version of a pancake

banana-cue: ripe banana pieces rolled in brown sugar and fried

banca: a small boat

bianbons: roasted banana mush

bolo: knife; Filipino equivalent of a machete

CAFGU: civilian deputized to help the Philippine troops

carabao: water buffalo

Cebuano: Filipino language

CR: "comfort room" (Filipino abbreviation for bathroom)

hajj: pilgrimage to Mecca prescribed as a religious duty to Muslims

halo-halo: crushed ice with sweetened condensed milk and mixed-in fruit

Ilocano: Filipino language

kalaw: duckbills—beautiful, big birds with bright red bills

langaw: from Tagalog for housefly—obligation to share something with others if they want it and ask for it

malong: wraparound skirt made of batik material

mujaheed (pl., mujahideen): fighter in Islamic holy war

pantos: pants (like pajama bottoms)

Sabaya: "booty of war"

*sabaya*ed: when a captive is "wedded" to a captor

"Salam!": "Peace!"

"Salam alaikom!": "Peace to you!"; standard greeting among Abu Sayyaf

sindol: hot coconut milk that can be mixed with fruit

sundalo: soldiers

Tagalog: Filipino language

terong: head covering, head shawl

tolda: multistriped plastic awning thrown over a rope between two trees for shade

tsinelas: flip-flops

viand: anything that goes on top of rice, such as a sauce

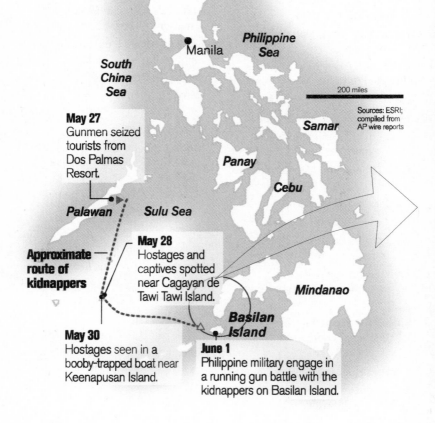

PHILIPPINES

Luzon

Manila

Philippine Sea

South China Sea

200 miles

Sources: ESRI; compiled from AP wire reports

Samar

May 27
Gunmen seized tourists from Dos Palmas Resort.

Panay

Cebu

Palawan   *Sulu Sea*

Approximate route of kidnappers

May 28
Hostages and captives spotted near Cagayan de Tawi Tawi Island.

Mindanao

May 30
Hostages seen in a booby-trapped boat near Keenapusan Island.

Basilan Island

June 1
Philippine military engage in a running gun battle with the kidnappers on Basilan Island.

Paul Soutar/*The Wichita Eagle*

Labason

Gutalac

Mindanao

Baliguian

Ipil

Friday's gun battle
between Philippine
soldiers and Abu Sayyaf
leaves Martin and Filipino
nurse dead, Gracia freed.

Siraway

Tungawan

Sulu Sea

Sibuco

Gracia taken to
hospital with
gunshot wound
to her leg.

PHILIPPINES

200 miles

KANSAS

25 miles

Zamboanga City

Basilan Strait

Basilan Island

Malamawi Island

Linungan Island

Baluc-Baluc Island

Isabela

Lamitan

Santa Clara

Maluso

Basilan Island

Bohelebung

Kaulungan Island

Tamuk Island

Amaloy

Mangal

Paul Soutar/*The Wichita Eagle*

Introduction

This is my story, but it's not my whole story. The whole story would take too long to write and would be too cumbersome to read. My coauthor, Dean Merrill, and I wrote and revised the manuscript and made cuts and more cuts. Unfortunately some of those cuts involved people who are near and dear to my heart, who worked incredibly hard to support me during and after my ordeal in the jungle. To these people I say, you were not left out because you aren't important. I hope you know what a special place you hold in my heart.

My goal in writing this has been to tell Martin's story. I hope we've done it well.

1

SEIZED AT DAWN

(May 27–28, 2001)

BANG, BANG, BANG!

Martin and I woke with a start. It was still dark outside and we couldn't see a thing. We could only hear the pounding on the wooden door of the beach cabin where we were celebrating our eighteenth wedding anniversary.

Bang, bang, bang, bang, bang!

Ugh—they want us to move to the next cabin, I thought. During dinner the night before, a member of the resort staff had said something vague about wanting us to change rooms but then had dropped the subject. I yelled to the person pounding on the door, "It's too early to move!"

Bang, bang, bang!

Martin yelled this time: "What?"

"It's a guard," came the reply.

I'll bet he's drunk, I thought, thinking that maybe the guard had been drinking during his overnight shift and was now out raising a ruckus. Once again, the banging resumed.

"Martin, I think the guard is drunk."

"No, I think something's wrong," he replied. He got up and started to head for the door.

"Honey, wait—you need to put some pants on first!"

Martin grabbed some knee-length khaki shorts, the kind with

baggy cargo pockets, from beside the bed. Meanwhile, I sat up and began to gather my clothes as well—a pair of shorts and a gray T-shirt I had worn the night before.

Just as Martin reached the door, it burst open. Three guys holding M16s charged into the room. All were short, and one was very young—probably in his teens. Another was perhaps twenty-three or twenty-four, with long black hair. I could tell the third man was somewhat older. All wore long-sleeved black shirts; two had camouflage pants. But there were no uniforms, no masks or sunglasses; we could see their faces.

Immediately, they swept Martin out the door, while the older man began yelling at me, "Go, go, go!"

"No, no, no!" I replied, clutching the sheet up around me. "I'm not dressed." I didn't know how much English he knew, but I was not about to obey him in my present state regardless. Shaking, I began pulling on my shorts.

"Okay, okay," he answered. I continued dressing.

One man had taken Martin outside, while the third one began to rifle through our belongings. He found our camera and our cell phone.

"Move, move, move!" came the order again. As I was hurried out the door, I grabbed our thong *tsinelas,* the common flip-flops that everyone wears in the Philippines. There wasn't time for me to grab my purse or anything else.

The young guy who followed me out wanted me to walk faster, even run. I knew from previous training that in the first few moments of a kidnapping, you're supposed to comply with orders in every way you can, until everybody's adrenaline calms down. But I was just so mad at this kid—I was *not* going to run!

"Faster, faster!" he said, jabbing me in the back with the barrel of his weapon.

With a calm voice I replied through clenched teeth, "I'm walking fast enough." I kept my pace. He jabbed me again, and it did hurt, but I was determined to exercise my will.

Once I got to the dock, a speedboat maybe thirty-five feet long with three massive outboard engines—the kind of boat used for drug running—was waiting. Four or five frightened hostages were already sitting on the floor of the boat. Martin, still shirtless, let out a sigh of relief to see me, having been forced to leave me in the room not fully clothed. "Oh, I'm so glad to see you," he said. "Did anybody hurt you?"

"No, no—I just had to get dressed."

Naturally, he was without his contact lenses, which made his vision a blur. Fortunately for me, he had encouraged me a couple of years earlier to have laser surgery on my eyes in Manila. So I was in good shape to see distances, even if he was not.

As I sat next to Martin in the boat, we watched as others began to arrive from the various cabins. Dawn was just starting to paint the eastern sky.

Some of the people started showing up with suitcases! One rather chic-looking couple came not only with suitcases but also with a big cooler of water. *My goodness,* I thought to myself, *I really didn't have to run out of the room so fast. I could have dragged my feet a little more and gotten some stuff together.*

I stood up and announced, "I'm going to go get Martin a shirt!"

"Sit down," barked one of the captors. "We'll get him a shirt."

I promptly obeyed. But I took notice of the fact that his English was quite good. *At least we can communicate with this one,* I thought. We later learned his name was Solaiman.

"I have our *tsinelas* here," I said to Martin, holding them up. I was really proud of myself.

"Yeah," he said. We didn't put them on our feet, however; we just held them. Martin was quiet as he looked around the boat, first at the men with guns and then at the other hostages. I could tell that he was trying to size up the situation, trying to figure it all out. This wasn't easy, however, since nearly everyone else on the boat was speaking languages we didn't understand. Occasionally, someone would throw an English word into the conversation and we'd be able to piece together some meaning. For the most part, however, we simply had to watch faces and listen to a person's tone of voice to figure out what he was saying.

I glanced down and the shine of my wedding ring caught my eye. *These guys are* not *going to get my ring!* I vowed. I pulled it off, along with a turquoise ring I was wearing on the other hand, and slipped them into my shorts pocket when no one was looking.

"Don't you think you should give me your wedding ring?" I asked Martin.

"Oh, no, we'll be fine," he answered, ever the optimist.

"Are you sure?"

"Yeah, it'll be okay."

• • •

This whole romantic getaway at Dos Palmas Resort had been my idea, a fact that weighed heavily on my mind as I sat there shivering in the boat. It came about after Martin was offered a promotion with New Tribes Mission, the group with whom we had served in mission aviation for more than fifteen years. The agency wanted him to become chief pilot for the entire organization, which would mean moving back to Arizona and overseeing all flight programs worldwide.

Although he was flattered by the offer, Martin really didn't want the position. "I just want to be what I've always been: a line pilot," he told me. Martin was never happier than when he was flying the mission's little red-and-white Cessna into jungle airstrips, bringing groceries and medicine to our missionary colleagues, or helping ferry tribal people out to medical appointments.

Nevertheless, Martin's extraordinary piloting and ability to work with people kept moving him higher and higher up the organization's chain of management. In fact, he had turned down this promotion several times because our three kids were still young and he didn't want to do all the required traveling.

I kept telling him, "You know, I don't want to move back to the States any more than you do. But the truth is, you're the right man for this position. You really are!" I loved the Philippines, but to be honest, I didn't care where we were or what we were doing, as long as we were together. Martin would just smile and shake his head at me.

About May 10, Martin left for a two-week trip to the United States so he could meet with the senior New Tribes leadership team. While he was away, the mission pilot on the western island of Palawan was called home due to a death in the family, leaving the island unmanned. Through e-mail, Martin and I concluded that as soon as he returned, Martin should go to Palawan to fill in; after all, the missionaries in the tribes needed flight service. Plus, a translator was already scheduled to come and do some tribal work on those particular days. He'd need a pilot.

As I went over Martin's schedule in my mind, I knew he would be returning to the Philippines tired and jet-lagged—and would immediately take off for a week's duty on Palawan. I also knew that he would put in long days on the island and that he'd have to cook for himself. It didn't seem right. I knew he needed help.

My schedule was packed as well, with visitors coming through— but then, oddly enough, a couple of things canceled. *I can go along with him and help him out,* I thought. Plus, with our wedding anniversary coming up on the twenty-eighth, if I went along I could at least be with him on that day. *Maybe we can even do something special while we're there. We've never had time to really enjoy the sights of Palawan.*

I called one of our coworkers on the island and asked her, "Where's a good place for Martin and me to celebrate our anniversary? He'll just be back from the States."

"Oooh, you should go to Dos Palmas," my friend said. "It's a wonderful resort on an island all its own; you can only get there by boat. The food is terrific, and they have two kinds of rooms— garden cottages on land and cottages on stilts over the water."

"What would you recommend?"

In the background I heard her husband call out, "Over the water! Those are the nice ones."

"Okay, why don't you go ahead and book one for us for Saturday night the twenty-sixth?" I said. After that, I arranged for our neighbors, Bob and Val Petro, to take care of the kids. I began cooking ahead and freezing some meals for them to eat while we were away.

When the Dos Palmas reservation came through, I looked at the price—10,000 pesos for the two of us ($200)—and got cold feet. Yes, it covered lodging, activities, and all meals, but still . . . that was an awful lot of money for our budget. Would Martin be upset with this extravagance? What would our donors think if they knew? *Maybe I should just call my friend back and ask if there's a nice place in town instead,* I thought.

If only I had . . .

• • •

I looked around and counted: there were seventeen hostages in all packed onto the floor of the speedboat. Up on the deck, ahead of the pilot wheel, a group of our captors stood, while a few others stood back by the motors. Conversation flowed, in both English and one or more other languages I didn't recognize.

The whole loading process had taken maybe twenty-five minutes—all the hostages had been taken from the cabins over the water, none from the garden cabins. At the last minute, somebody said, "Wait! We need a cook." Quickly, one of the kidnappers jumped out of the boat and ran up to the top of the hill to abduct the resort's cook; his name was Sonny. Two security guards were nabbed as well. Obviously, they were no match for the raiders.

With Sonny and the guards, our hostage count rose to twenty.

The engines powered up, we pulled away from the pier—and suddenly one mystery was solved. The entire group of fifteen or so captors began to pump their fists in the air as they chorused in unison, *"Allah akbar! Allah akbar!* [Allah is the greatest! Allah is the greatest!]" Instantly, we knew who we were dealing with: the dreaded Abu Sayyaf. They were the only ones with the audacity to do something like this.

I didn't know a lot about the Abu Sayyaf, other than that they were terrorists. Throughout the southern Philippines, people were afraid of them. We learned later the meaning of their name, which set the tone accurately: *Abu* ("father of") *Sayyaf* ("the swordsman").

This was the same group that had taken Jeffrey Schilling, an African-American Muslim who had come to the Philippines to marry a Muslim girl the year before. Upon hearing about the Abu Sayyaf, he thought he could go to them, as a fellow Muslim, and explain that their tactics violated the Koran. His attempts at reeducation backfired immediately; they said he was a CIA agent, turned him into a hostage, and demanded one million dollars in ransom. Jeffrey was held for seven and a half months. We had heard he finally escaped by slipping out of his handcuffs, made possible by his weight loss.

I turned to Martin with a heaviness starting to press down upon my shoulders. "We are in big trouble," I said.

"Yeah, we are," he quietly agreed.

I watched as the white cabins of Dos Palmas grew tiny on the receding horizon, and soon I couldn't see any land at all. We roared out into the Sulu Sea, heading who knew where? The ride across the open water grew rough, and we found ourselves bouncing into the air and slamming down onto the floor again and again. The boat was seriously overloaded with thirty-five bodies aboard. We bumped ahead regardless.

I wasn't crying or shaky yet; all that would come later. I was steeling myself to stay calm, trying to stay focused as each event unfolded. I was also working to recall a class I had taken back in the late 1980s, when New Tribes Mission had sent their contingency planner, Guy Sier, to prepare the missionary team for hostage situations.

"The first few moments, when everyone is being rounded up,"

he had said, "is when the captors are the most trigger-happy. So do what you're told. But soon after that, begin to make eye contact with your kidnappers. Start to become a real person to them, not just an item. Go ahead and let them know what your needs are. That helps establish your individuality in their minds."

What else had he said? I hadn't really been paying full attention that day, and neither had Martin. Kidnapping was something that happened to other people, not to us.

I decided to put into practice the part I remembered. When the driver throttled back just a bit, I caught Solaiman's eye and announced with a firm voice, "We need a CR [the Philippine abbreviation for 'comfort room,' or bathroom]." After all, we'd all been pulled out of our beds and hustled straight onto the boat. "Where can we go?"

"Yeah, yeah," the other hostages agreed, nodding.

"There's no CR here," Solaiman declared.

That wasn't good enough for me. "Well, we need to go to the bathroom, so we're gonna go," I retorted. I got up and headed for the stern of the boat.

One of the other hostages volunteered to hold up a *malong* (the big Philippine wraparound skirt made of batik material) to give us women a bit of privacy as we squatted, one after another, right on the floor. When this process was complete, the engines powered up again, and we were off.

As we sped through the sea, the spray of salt water came flying over us from time to time, leaving us drenched and chilled. An older man began to visibly shake with cold, and someone passed him a shirt to wear.

A young woman sitting near me was scared out of her wits. I began talking with her and learned that her name was Divine. She looked at me with terror in her eyes and said, "Our family has no money for ransom! We don't have anything!"

I put my hand on her shoulder and said, "You know, it doesn't matter if you have money or not. Money won't do any good right now anyway. The Lord's the only one we can trust. Try to calm down, and let's just think about getting through today."

She clung to my hand and seemed to settle down a little.

About an hour into the trip, one of the older Abu Sayyaf leaders, Mang Ben, a bearded man in his thirties, leaned over toward Martin. Looking down at Martin's hand, he announced with a stately air, "I want that ring!"

Martin could do nothing but hand it over.

I looked at my husband and whispered, "What did I tell you?" I couldn't help remembering the day when I had bought that simple gold band. I'd paid fifty dollars for it at Service Merchandise in Raytown, Missouri, outside Kansas City. Now it had been stolen in broad daylight. I tried to remind myself that we could get another ring. *It's just a gold ring,* I told myself. *A ring can be replaced.* I gripped Martin's hand even more tightly.

Occasionally, another boat would come into view on the horizon. Whenever this happened, the captors herded us together so they could cover us with a tarpaulin in order not to be noticed. During one of these times, we heard the engines throttle back, and another boat came alongside. A conversation ensued in a language I couldn't understand. Apparently it had to do with getting food, because the other crew tossed the Abu Sayyaf some kind of packet.

Once the boat left, the food was passed under the tarp to us. It was cassava, something I'd never eaten before, although I knew it was grown by some Philippine farmers. I later learned that cassava is poisonous if eaten raw, but it can be peeled, boiled, and then drained for eating. Or it can be pounded, mixed with water, and put into banana leaves for steaming. It comes out like a hard paste.

My first bite was very vinegary. "Is this okay to eat?" I asked.

"Oh, yes," one of the other hostages replied. "In fact, once it's fixed like this, it can last for days and days."

I hadn't realized how hungry and thirsty I was until we began to share the cassava. The couple who had brought the big water jug passed it around so the rest of us could have a drink. That helped a little—but I couldn't help but think about the delicious peanut M&M's I'd left in the room, and I mourned the loss.

As the day progressed, the sun grew hot and the tarp was rigged up to provide some shade. The captors said nothing about where we were headed. We studied them, trying to figure out their names and who were the bosses. One of the men quickly stood out for his colorful personality and ability to turn a phrase. Sabaya was short and stocky. While everyone else wore army fatigues or baggy pants, Sabaya wore tight red stretch pants, looking oddly out of place.

We found out later that his name, and most of the others', were not their given ones but rather their "jihad names," chosen to evoke their new personas for battle. Sabaya, for example, meant "booty of war." Other names had equally vivid meanings, of which they were very proud.

Around two or three in the afternoon, Solaiman came to the group of hostages with a Big Chief pad of yellow paper to start interviewing us. He began by saying, "We're the Abu Sayyaf. Some people call us terrorists. We want you to know, we're not terrorists. We are simply people whom the Philippine government has robbed of our homeland, and we just want it back. No one in the government will listen to us, and so we have to do things like this to gain notice."

He asked us our names and what our jobs were. One by one, he wrote down the information:

- Francis, an older gentleman and banker, and his wife, Tess
- Chito, a sales representative with a cell-phone company, and his coworker Janice
- Reggie, who was well connected to the power circles of Manila, and his girlfriend, Rizza. This was the couple who had brought the suitcases and the water jug.
- Buddy, a publisher of a travel-guide magazine (for which he had been scouting an article on Dos Palmas), his wife, Divine, and their eight-year-old son, R. J.

- Angie, Divine's sister, a young woman who appeared to be in her early thirties
- Guillermo Sobero, an American contractor, and Fe, his young fiancée
- Letty, a Chinese businesswoman, and her daughter, Kim, who was perhaps thirteen or fourteen, plus Letty's niece, Lalaine, also a young teenager. Lalaine had been staying in the garden cottages with her own family but had gone down to the water to spend Saturday night with her aunt and cousin.
- Sonny, the Dos Palmas cook
- Eldren and Armando, the two Dos Palmas guards
- Martin and me

Except for Guillermo, Martin, and me, all were Philippine citizens and well-off enough to afford a place like Dos Palmas.

When Solaiman got to us, Martin replied, "We're American missionaries with a group called New Tribes Mission. We try to help the tribal people. We live up on Luzon."

A cloud of disappointment came across Solaiman's face. He had hoped that we would be European—or at least American—business types, whose company would readily pay to get us back. Mission groups, on the other hand, were *(a)* poor and *(b)* on record with standing policies against ever paying ransom.

"Missionaries? Did you know Charles Walton?" he asked. We did. Charles was an SIL (Wycliffe Bible) translator who had been taken hostage on the island of Mindanao some ten years earlier. He eventually got out alive, but not before spending weeks in a cramped cage up off the ground.

May 27
2:00 A.M., Rose Hill, Kansas: The phone rings in Martin's parents' bedroom with news that their son and daughter-in-law have been kidnapped.

"Yes, we know him," Martin replied. "He's a friend; he works for an organization much like ours."

"Well, some of us were there," Solaiman answered, with a touch of mystery.

Then he returned to our case with this ominous announcement: "Yours will be a political ransom. We will make demands, and we will deal with you last."

Uh-oh, I thought to myself. *We're going to be in this a long time.* I immediately thought of the promise I had made to the kids: "Dad and I will be on Palawan for just a week, and then we'll be back home again." I felt sick at heart, trying to imagine how they would feel when they learned what had happened to us. I leaned toward Martin and murmured, "How long did they hold those Sipadan people?" referring to a group of twenty-one tourists captured the year before from a resort in Malaysia.

"I can't remember. Three, four months?"

I tried to guess in my mind what "a long time" would actually be. Six weeks? I tentatively set my hopes on two months at the very outside. *Worst-case scenario, we'll spend the summer with these guys and be out by the time the kids go back to school,* I told myself.

Meanwhile, the other hostages were already busy figuring out how much money they could raise. It seemed that everybody knew this was the name of the game. Muslim advancement may have been the announced overall goal, but cash was the necessary fuel. The bargaining was in full swing.

"Maybe my family could come up with one million [pesos, or $20,000]," said one person.

A more middle-class fellow said, "We might be able to raise 250,000 [$5,000]."

Solaiman kept writing down the amounts. (We learned later that this was the first time he had been allowed to handle these negotiations, and Sabaya was not happy with how it had gone. "You don't let them set the amounts," he told Solaiman. "You just look at them, size them up, and tell them how much to pay. If they have a Chinese last name, that means they're wealthy, so—10 million pesos [$200,000], end of discussion.")

After Solaiman worked through the list, the conversation ended. The engine roared, and we moved on.

At one point that afternoon, Solaiman said to Martin, "You know, people think we're a third-rate, primitive group out here. Actually, we're very modern, high-tech. See our satellite phone? See our GPS? We know what we're doing!"

(I couldn't help smiling, however, at the fact that somehow the Global Positioning System device hadn't helped them very much in finding our resort. We had pieced together their conversations enough to know that on their trip to Dos Palmas, they had gotten lost and had had to ask a fisherman for directions. Obviously they didn't know how to use their GPS!)

I kept scanning the horizon for land. None appeared. Everywhere I looked, I saw open sea. I now know that the nearest islands of any size were more than three hundred miles to the southeast. It was probably better for me not to know that at the time.

After a full day of bouncing across the water, we were terribly sore. At sundown, we came up to a larger fishing boat. Here, another ten to twenty Abu Sayyaf, plus the fishing crew, were waiting. We joined them. We were relieved to get off the speedboat. At least we would be able to stand up without being jarred onto the floor. We hoped this move would be more comfortable for us.

A bamboo "lead" no more than five inches wide was laid down from the speedboat up to the fishing boat, and I realized I was going to have to walk across maybe eight feet of open water to get there. It scared me to death. *I can't do this!* I thought.

The water below swelled gently as I stared at the bamboo. When

---

May 27
Paul and Oreta Burnham ask New Tribes Mission personnel in Manila to evacuate the children to their home in Rose Hill, per Martin and Gracia's standing instruction.

---

it was my turn, I admitted I had no choice. I began to crawl across the void on my hands and knees, praying that I would not fall.

Martin came right behind me, and by the time we all piled aboard, there were close to sixty people—again, a far greater load than this seventy-five-foot craft was ever meant to carry.

The boat had an inboard engine and outriggers—bamboo poles lashed together to make extensions off the sides. The pilot wheel was inside a small cabin in the middle of the deck. Down in the hold were large tunas packed in ice, fish the crew had caught before being hijacked by the Abu Sayyaf a few moments earlier.

We sat down on the deck while the captors quickly began their evening prayers. As the chants washed over the boat, I felt my mind slipping into a fog. *I can't believe this is happening.* When they finished with their prayers, we ate some rice and tuna, which helped a bit. But again, there was no place for the women to go to the bathroom. Again, we were forced to use a corner. Angie, Fe, and some of the other women were distraught and crying.

"Do you think people know yet that we've been captured?" I asked Martin as the darkness grew around us.

"It's hard to tell," he said. "But don't worry, Gracia. We're gonna be okay." His optimism was contagious.

A song I'd heard the previous week began to run through my head. "Martin, I heard this song while you were away. Try to sleep and I'll sing it to you." I began to quietly repeat the melody:

> *Be strong, be strong, be strong in the Lord,*
> *And be of good courage for he is your guide.*
> *Be strong, be strong, be strong in the Lord,*
> *And rejoice for the victory is yours.**

"Mmmm, that's a good song," Martin murmured when I finished. "Thank you, honey."

Nobody really stretched out to sleep that first night; we all

*BE STRONG IN THE LORD by Linda Lee Johnson © 1979 Hope Publishing Company, Carol Stream, IL 60188. All rights reserved. Used by permission.

just sat up and dozed, leaning on one another from time to time. It turned cold, as ocean breezes began to replace the heat of the day. Solaiman's earlier promise to get Martin a shirt had produced nothing, so Francis gave him a sleeveless one to wear. We huddled together for warmth.

Sleep was fitful. I remember waking once to find that my head had fallen down to the deck, and somebody's foot was on my hair. I jerked it loose.

• • •

The next morning was Monday—Memorial Day in the States, but hardly a holiday for us. When the sun came up, we explored the boat to see what we had missed in the twilight before. Someone made a "CR" for us—a platform out on the bamboo outrigger with a tarp curtain around it. Getting out there was still tricky, but there was a rope to hold, and at least we could go in the ocean rather than on the boat's floor.

People got busy on the satellite phone, calling their relatives in Manila and elsewhere to arrange ransom payments. Impassioned discussions ensued. Reggie showed his connections right away, getting a government official to call Sabaya back and say, "I know this guy, and he's a good guy. Let him out, since you owe me a favor, remember?" They agreed on an amount of money to be transferred, and Reggie's release was promised.

By this time, Guillermo was definitely showing signs of stress. He was on a lot of medication due to a recent nervous breakdown, he explained, adding something about being overwhelmed by a messy divorce that wasn't yet finalized. Now we could see him going through withdrawal. His body quivered from time to time, and his voice was shaky.

This boat was certainly slower than the speedboat had been. "Where are we headed?" one of the hostages asked.

The answer from the Abu Sayyaf was vague: "We'll just see...."

I was painfully aware that I wasn't dressed properly for the Muslim standard. Of course, they hadn't given me time back in the room to do anything better. Other women were still in their pajamas. I sat there feeling embarrassed that, in their minds, I was just another typical "loose" American woman in my shorts and T-shirt. I began asking the Lord to protect me.

Sometime that morning Fe gave me a long piece of lace for a *terong* (head covering), and someone else threw me a *malong*. Although my bare arms were still showing, I was at least somewhat more presentable to Muslim eyes.

Solaiman wanted us to know that we were in an atmosphere of high morals. "Would we ever lie to you? No. Would we ever steal from you? No. Would we ever touch the women? Never. The Koran forbids these things." He began to rhapsodize about how great it is when Allah is the ruler and the Koran is the guidebook— as in Afghanistan, their cherished model. "Afghanistan will show the world how great the truly Islamic state can be. You know, in Islam, if you're a thief, they cut off your hand. That's how things ought to be."

I thought to myself, *Wait a minute—didn't you guys just steal Martin's wedding ring?!*

"In Islam, all the women are dressed properly, with nothing showing but their eyes. If a lady's eyes are causing a scandal, even they will be covered. There are no enticements to sin, no Western movies, no drinking, no smoking, no drugs."

Our captors' greatest goal, it seemed, was to get to Afghanistan. What a utopia that would be, they said. But if that didn't work out,

---

May 27
Lynn Burggraf, New Tribes missionary and close family friend, is assigned to break the bad news to the Burnham children—Jeff, Mindy, and Zach.

---

they would settle for their second choice: to go to America and get a good job!

At some point that day, Sabaya asked Martin to get on the sat-phone and make a statement to Radyo Agong in Mindanao. This radio station, we eventually learned, was friendly to Abu Sayyaf interests and willing to air their messages when asked.

So Martin prepared to speak; the voice would be his, but the script came from Sabaya, of course:

> I, Martin Burnham, along with my wife, Gracia, who have lived in the Philippines for fifteen years, members of New Tribes Mission, have been taken hostage by the Abu Sayyaf, the Janjalani group. . . .

Actually, Sabaya wanted him to say *Al-Harakatul Islamia,* which means "the Islamic Movement," but Martin was afraid he would blow the pronunciation.

"Okay, then just call us 'the Osama bin Laden group,'" Sabaya said.

Here in late May 2001, a full three months before September 11, that name meant nothing to me. Martin told me later that he had heard it once or twice.

"Can I just say 'the Janjalani group,' because I know that term, and I won't get tripped up?" Martin asked, referring to the group's founder, who had died in battle a couple of years before. Approval was granted. His speech continued:

> We appeal to the American and Philippine governments to work to bring this situation to a peaceful end very soon.

As usual, Martin kept his cool, talking very calmly without notes. When he finished, he came over to me.

"You did a good job, honey," I said. "You always do."

Near the end of the day, Chito, who was full of life and spunk, decided to organize a "getting to know you" exercise for his fellow hostages. We all crowded into the wheelhouse and sat around on the floor or whatever else we could find. Going around the circle, each person gave his or her name and the person's name to the left. Soon we all had one another's names nailed down. We talked and even laughed together a bit, trying to make the best of the situation. We talked about our interests and other personal things.

Guillermo told us he'd been born in Peru but had immigrated as a teenager to the Los Angeles area, where he now had a small construction business. He had come to Dos Palmas on vacation the year before, which is when he had met Fe working in the gift shop. They had been in touch by e-mail ever since, and now they were engaged.

As we learned bits and pieces about each of the other hostages, we became more of a team, more willing to encourage one another and try to keep our spirits up.

By that evening, the "ecumenical" nature of the boat was in full evidence. The Muslims, of course, conducted their ritual of bowing down and praying as they faced west, toward Mecca. The Catholics got out their rosary beads. Finally, one of the hostages asked Martin to pray aloud for the benefit of the group.

"Lord, all of this doesn't surprise you," he began in a calming voice as we all bowed our heads. "You know where we are, even though we don't. We know that people are worried about us. But you hold us in your hands. Give us the grace to go through this trial. We're depending on you. Amen."

A peace settled into my heart as I listened to my husband's

May 28
Philippine president Gloria Arroyo appears on national television to declare "all-out war" on the Abu Sayyaf, telling them she will "finish what you have started."

May 28
Martin's sister, Cheryl Spicer, and her husband, Walt, drive seven hours north from Manila to Aritao to stay with the Burnham children.

---

words. The same seemed to happen for the others. "Wow, you can really pray good!" they said. Martin laughed. For him, prayer was just his way of talking to God, sharing the thoughts of his heart.

By that night, we had generally figured out where we'd all like to sleep. The younger members of the Abu Sayyaf had already staked out the roof of the wheelhouse as theirs. Near the bow were places to hang hammocks, which were claimed by their comrades. A few others rigged up hammocks near the back. The fishing crew claimed their turf.

As for the hostages, we mostly stacked ourselves along the narrow sides of the deck, heads inward and feet hanging out over the ocean. A few others settled into a central well space in front of the wheelhouse. All together, we covered every inch of available space.

There was one luxury about these circumstances, I noticed: No mosquitoes! They had nowhere to breed here in the midst of salt water. We could lie out here and stare at the stars above without being bitten. There was a gentle breeze, and the sound of the water lapping against the boat sounded peaceful.

Francis and Tess, as it turned out, were fans of the old Beatles music, and in fact, they sang quite well together. As we stretched out under the open sky, they began to sing the mellow songs: "Yesterday," "Ticket to Ride," "Let It Be," "The Long and Winding Road." The rest of us joined in when we could. Even the Abu Sayyaf sang a little, though such music was technically forbidden by their faith.

Then we came to the song "Imagine," John Lennon's ballad about a different world. When we got to the line "Imagine all the people, living life in peace" I finally lost it. For the first time since we'd been kidnapped, tears began to stream down my face. It was so poignant—all these hostages singing about a world so near and yet so unbelievably beyond our grasp. As we lay there in that moment, a bond began to form, connecting us with one another, even our captors. Looking up at the sky, I found myself drifting into ragged sleep.

2
BRIGHT BEGINNINGS

(1959–81)

LEARNING TO GET ALONG in crowded conditions was a skill I had acquired early, as the fifth child of six in the Norvin and Betty Jo Jones household. In fact, I was born just as my parents were recovering from the tragic loss of my oldest sister, Terry Lynn. Only nine years old, she had been cut down by a reckless motorist who had, on June 10, 1958, ignored a bus's flashing lights and arm signal and pulled around it anyway.

I was in the womb at the time. My mother told me later that being pregnant forced her to keep going from day to day, to eat properly, and not to sink into abject despair. I arrived at St. Mary's Hospital in Cairo, Illinois, on January 17, 1959.

They named me Gracia (pronounced *"gray*-sha"). We moved a year later so my father could pastor a church in Ripley, Tennessee. Then in 1962, he was asked to help start a Bible college in Woodstock, Ontario, which is where my memories begin. My baby sister, Mary, was born there. I went to school in Woodstock, and of course I learned to ice-skate there. In my little pink-and-gray leggings outfit, I would fall time and time again, but no matter how many times I hit the ice, I always got up again.

It was a wonderful childhood in so many ways. In addition to Mary, I had two other sisters, Becky and Nancy, and one brother, Paul. We always seemed to get along well, thanks to our parents' wise guidance. They put the Lord and his Word at the center of our lives. I could sing hymns from memory even before I could read, although not always with full comprehension. I puzzled for quite a while over the song "Bringing in the 'Cheese' " (instead of "Sheaves"), until someone finally enlightened me.

Our family was in church every time the doors were open: Sunday school, morning services, evening services, midweek prayer services, plus the assorted dinners and special events that always seemed to come up.

When I was seven or eight, I had a wonderful Sunday school teacher who explained to me the importance of committing my life to Christ. Not long after that, I remember begging for the opportunity to be baptized.

When I was a little older, the Bible college moved northwest to Sault Ste. Marie, where it was really cold. All four of us girls had to share one bedroom, using two sets of bunk beds. Somehow we stayed warm through the long, dark winter that year. A year later, my father accepted a pastorate in southeastern Illinois, at Congregational Christian Church in Olney. I started fifth grade in Olney and built many friendships that I've maintained to this day.

Somewhere around the house I picked up a book about Amy Carmichael, the young Irish woman who went to India around the turn of the twentieth century to work with children. She found out that little girls were being forced into prostitution in the Hindu temples, and she set up a refuge to shelter them. Her writings over the next fifty years of her life were profound and inspiring.

Even more vivid in my imagination was the Scottish missionary Mary Slessor, who was the subject of another book I must have read half a dozen times. Mary worked in Africa—specifically, Nigeria—a little before the time of Amy Carmichael. There she battled witchcraft, cannibalism, alcoholism, and the particularly gruesome practice of killing newborn twins because they were supposedly a bad omen. What I liked about Mary Slessor was that she was gutsy; she'd stand up to tribal chiefs and tell them exactly what she thought! They didn't quite know what to do with her.

At this point I had no conscious thought of ever becoming a missionary myself. But I found these biographies inspiring.

Our family moved once more when I was fifteen and Dad became a professor of Bible and theology at Calvary Bible College in Kansas City. My sister Mary and I attended a private academy called Tri-City Christian School, from which I graduated in 1977. This gave me the chance to expand not only my love of music but also my first and best talent: socializing. I really liked planning and organizing parties and events, both at church and at school. I loved being around people and always wanted to make sure everyone was having a good time. My friend Diane Jaeger and I would often arrive at class to comments of "We heard you coming!"

When I wasn't doing homework, I managed to sing, play basketball and soccer, help with fund-raisers, meet yearbook deadlines, and be a cheerleader—such wonderful days.

I applied to and was accepted by several colleges, but the thing that hooked me on Calvary Bible College was its music program. Peter Friesen, the greatest choir director I'd ever met, gave me voice lessons even before I enrolled as a freshman. I fell in love with his instruction, and soon I was enveloped in the busy swirl of college life.

My first roommate was Marcia Miller. We were both poor, and the cafeteria didn't operate on weekends. So we'd scrape our money together and walk to Wendy's to order a single Frosty. At the condiment rack where you pick up your spoon, we'd also pick up some crackers that were supposed to go with chili . . . only we would sit and dip them in our Frosty in order to make a meal. (That's probably not what the Wendy's corporation had in mind.)

I learned a lot from watching Marcia's spiritual walk with God. She inspired me to live a simple, genuine faith. She taught me to look for God's hand in even the smallest daily events.

Believe it or not, I did love to study. But even more than that,

I loved the social life. I got involved in about everything there was: singing alto in choir as well as a small ensemble that traveled on weekends, teaching fourth-grade Sunday school at Tri-City Baptist Church, visiting a detention center once a week to counsel kids who had gotten in trouble with the law. Eventually I became the yearbook editor, student council secretary, a resident assistant on the freshman girls' floor—and in between, I worked in the snack shop to pay my school bill. It was crazy, but I loved every minute of it.

Even when my parents moved away to northeast Arkansas to take a pastorate and be near my grandmother, I knew I wanted to stay at Calvary. At that time, Calvary was located in a former nunnery with a beautiful chapel. My friend Margie and I would go in there at odd moments and sit where the acoustics were just right, then sing every song we knew.

Another friend, Kathy Stech, had a car, which gave the rest of us some mobility. By my senior year, I had yet another close friend, Elizabeth Redden, who was dating a really cute guy named Doug Burnham. I didn't know much about him, except that he was sort of quiet and an "MK" (missionary kid) from the Philippines. Even though Doug was quiet, everyone on campus seemed to know who he was. Soon after returning from Christmas break my senior year, Elizabeth said to me, "Hey, did you know that Doug's older brother is transferring here for the second semester? His name is Martin, and I guess he's already had some pilot training, because they're going to let him teach in the flight program as well as go to classes himself. He'll be a junior. Do you want to meet him?"

Sure, why not? I thought. *If he's as cute as Doug, this could be a worthwhile conversation.* She guided me over to a lunch table where the two brothers were eating. Martin was a handsome guy with hair a little darker than Doug's, more reddish than blond. "Hi, guys!" said Elizabeth. "How's the spaghetti today?"

She introduced me and we made some small talk. Our

conversation didn't last long. As we walked away to head for our afternoon schedules, I remember thinking that Martin seemed just as nice as his brother.

As the semester rolled along, I was busy, of course, getting ready to graduate. Even though we didn't know each other well, Martin and I always seemed to be in the same place. He seemed really nice, and he ran with a crowd of guys I enjoyed—fun-loving, casual guys in their jeans and flannel shirts, not out to impress anybody. Martin even wore cowboy boots. Whereas a lot of the other male students seemed fascinated with designer clothes and ties, wanting to look like they were headed somewhere important in the world, Martin and his friends would rather be wearing "kick-back clothes." Some of them were pilots in training, some were farm boys, and all were down-to-earth. I liked that.

Graduation day, when I received my bachelor's degree with a major in Christian education, was special, of course. My older sister Nancy surprised me by coming along with my parents. After the ceremony, my sister-in-law, Beth, hosted a lovely luncheon for the whole family.

The college had already offered me a job as secretary to the student-services group—the dean of students, the dean of men, the dean of women, and the chaplain. I was glad for this chance, not only because it would pay the bills but also because I'd get to stay at Calvary, a place I loved. Kathy Stech and I rented a small, roach-infested apartment nearby, and we enjoyed being on our own; even the bugs didn't daunt us. By August I was settled into my desk at one end of the administration building, juggling the needs of four busy people as they organized their programs for the fall semester.

As the semester began, it became apparent that one of the men's dorms housed a number of especially rowdy guys. Its resident assistant, whose job was to keep a lid on things, was Martin. Time and again he would show up at my desk with one of his charges in tow, summoned to face the dean and explain the latest antics. This gave

Martin and me chances to sit and talk while waiting for the ominous door to open.

He talked about his classes and about his folks far away in the
Philippines, serving a tribe called the Ibaloi. He told me he was the
oldest of five children; besides Doug, there were Cheryl and Brian,
who were both in high school in Manila. And then there was his little
sister, Felicia, still a preschooler. He said one day, "Did you know
I had to help my mom sew up my leg one day after I cut it with a
machete?" (All boys in the Philippine rain forest carry a machete.)
That's when I learned that his mother was a nurse.

Understandably, he was very involved with the Missionary
Prayer Fellowship (MPF), a student organization that focused on
world outreach. He and his friend Clay Bowlin planned weekly
meetings to focus on various populations overseas and their spiritual needs. They prayed for missionaries—many of them Calvary
alumni—serving all around the globe.

When it came time for the annual MPF chapel service, Martin
and Clay put together a drama highlighting various mission pio-
neers through the centuries.

Martin played William Carey of England, the first modern-
era missionary. Dressed in full Georgian costume, complete with
knickers, he began in his rich, baritone voice:

> As a young child I learned the importance of putting my
> best effort into all that I did, and completing each task that
> I started—a discipline that was to pay off in my later years on
> the mission field. . . .
>
> From the beginning God gave me the desire to know
> exactly what his Word said. . . . As I continued my study and
> meditation on his Word, I could not help but be impressed
> with the fact that we, as believers, were simply not doing all
> that God had commanded.
>
> When his Word says, "Go ye," he means *Go ye!* And when
> he says, "into all the world," he means into *all* the world. To

"preach the gospel to every creature" means exactly that. God means exactly what he says.

He has commanded us to "go and make disciples of all nations." The promise that follows is "lo, I am with you always." Do any of us have the right to play leapfrog with the command and [only] hug to the promise?

I didn't know it at the time, but Martin could have been describing his own upbringing, his study of the Scriptures, and his personal passion as well as William Carey's. The bigger perspective had already taken root in his soul.

On another occasion, MPF staged *Through Gates of Splendor,* the tragic story of the five missionaries massacred in 1956 by warriors of an indigenous tribe in Ecuador. We all knew the story, of course, since it had gotten so much press. But even so, we sat there riveted as the five men waited on the sandbar of the river beside their little mission plane, expecting the Aucas to return for another friendly conversation like the day before.

One of the actors jumped up and pointed toward the imaginary jungle. "Oh, good!" he cried. "Here they come again!"

And then his face froze. "But look—they've got their blowguns with them. . . ."

The play ended abruptly. The actors didn't need to show what happened next; we all knew.

I stood up to leave the chapel that day, unable to say a word. *Will the Lord ever require me to do what those men did? to go through what they went through?* I was stunned. I slowly headed out the door, tears streaming down my face.

3
THE NICEST GUY
(1981–83)

My DATING LIFE THAT FALL was not going well. I had been in a relationship with someone whom I deeply cared about, but it was becoming clear to me that a long-term commitment was not in our future. After much anguish and discussion with my friends, I finally mustered the courage to break it off.

I was devastated. As I approached my twenty-third birthday, my future was nothing but a haze. One afternoon, Martin stopped in the office. After some small talk, he smiled and said, "The fall concert is coming up, and I wonder if you'd like to go with me."

I was standing by the typewriter, and my face went white. (At least that's what he claimed later.) I slowly sat down and said, "Oh . . . are you asking me for a date?"

"Yeah."

All kinds of thoughts swirled through my head. *Do I want to get into all this again? What if it ends up like the last time? I don't want to be hurt again.*

Finally, I got out the words "Can I let you know?"

What I had no way of knowing was that Martin had heard that same line from other girls so often, in fact, that he was tired of it. He had convinced himself that the line was simply a way for them to put him off until they could decline his offer later, either in a note or through a friend.

So he had decided that if he heard "Can I let you know?" one more time, he would call the girl's bluff and retract his invitation.

When I said the dreaded line, Martin steeled himself to say, "No, you can't. Never mind."

But for some inexplicable reason it came out, "Yeah. You can let me know"! With that, he turned and headed off to class.

The instant he left the building, I dashed into the office of my friends Kay and Joyce.

"Hey, guess who just asked me out?" I bubbled to Joyce. "Martin Burnham!"

"Oh, really!" they responded with big grins. *Everyone* liked Martin. He was just such a nice guy.

"Should I do this?"

"Of course! Of course!" They encouraged me to go for it.

I returned to my desk and quickly pulled out a notecard embossed with roses that I had on hand. I wrote:

Thank you for asking me [out] for Saturday night. It really encouraged me. I would love to go with you. Stop back by and we'll talk about the time.

I sent it over to the flight department with the very next person headed that way.

That weekend, I went out and bought a new dress for the occasion, even though I rarely spent money on clothes for myself. I chose a beautiful yellow dress that had spaghetti straps and a lacy jacket.

On Saturday evening, we double-dated with another couple. During the concert, I looked down and saw that despite his suit, Martin had on cowboy boots. I got this big smile on my face.

Martin caught my expression and said, "What?"

"Oh, nothing," I replied. I didn't want him to think I was criticizing his outfit. It wasn't that I thought it was funny, actually. It just confirmed to me that he was his own person—that he wasn't going to let the laws of social etiquette dictate to him. I liked that.

After the concert, he took us flying to see the lights of Kansas City at night. As a resident assistant, he needed to be back at the dorm by a certain time, but we used every minute before Martin delivered me home.

We started dating more after that, and I quickly came to appreciate Martin's unassuming ways. If he wanted to be the life of the party, he could. But if someone else was playing that role, he could just as easily be one of the guys. There was nothing egotistical about him. He was very confident in his talents, but he didn't have to tell you about them. Instead, he was just quietly competent, and he was always kind to everybody in the process.

He had a cool car—a green Chevelle. He would let me drive it, which was quite a step up from my little Datsun B210 that needed to be overhauled. Bless his heart—when I told him about my car, he took it into the school shop and overhauled it himself, with some help from a friend.

• • •

The more we got to know one another, the more I learned of his interesting past. When he was a little guy, his family had attended Wichita Bible Church, a strong mission-minded congregation that held a one-week missions conference every October. The year Martin was seven, a guest speaker from New Tribes Mission made a deep impression on his parents, Paul and Oreta Burnham. Paul worked for a chemical plant and Oreta was a nurse. They already had four young children, but they began to wonder if maybe God had different ideas for them other than staying in central Kansas the rest of their lives.

The following spring, they attended a five-day New Tribes conference in Wisconsin for missionary prospects. Paul's dad paid for the two plane tickets, while Oreta's parents babysat. They came home more challenged than ever to venture toward overseas ministry—enough that they put their house on the market. It sold quickly, providing the funds for a year of training.

Some people said they were crazy to attempt this, given the size of their family and the fact that they were already in their thirties. But off they went to Wisconsin in their six-year-old Chevrolet packed with kids and clothes and lots of home-canned green beans. To young Martin and his siblings, it was all a great adventure. He understood what it meant to give your life to the Lord's work, having made his own personal commitment to Christ back in a first-grade Sunday school class.

After a year of training in Wisconsin, the family headed to Camdenton, Missouri, for another year of language school. By the end of their training, the house-sale proceeds were running out. The Burnhams moved back to the family roots in the small town of Rose Hill, Kansas, just east of Wichita, where Paul took odd jobs to put bread on the table while he talked to churches about supporting their missions dream. And so it happened that in the summer of 1970, they boarded a freighter called the *Philippine Corregidor* in San Francisco's harbor for the monthlong voyage across the wide Pacific. Martin was now ten years old.

Martin played hide-and-seek with his brothers between stacks of zinc ingots on the deck of the ship. The boys had fun flying kites off the stern and watching the flying fish alongside the railing as they soared for amazing distances.

When the family finally docked in Manila Bay, they were immediately struck by the hot and steamy climate. They were also surprised at how much English they heard. The American presence in the country for fifty years had made a difference. While Filipinos do speak Tagalog and Cebuano and Ilocano, English is the language that seems to tie them all together.

Since there appeared to be no practical way for Martin to attend school in the tribal area where his parents were working (homeschooling had not yet flowered into the option that it is today), he was sent to boarding school. He didn't want to be away from his family, but the fact that he could fly home occasionally on a mission plane made dormitory life easier to take. It was on these flights home that Martin first found his fascination with airplanes and flying.

Mission aviation was not a luxury but rather a necessity in rural areas of the Philippines, where roads were few and rough, and waterways constantly blocked travel. New Tribes Mission, which specializes in working with indigenous people groups, was extremely dependent on the pilots who ferried groceries, medicines, mail, equipment, and people from town to short jungle airstrips. Paul and Oreta Burnham, for example, were a two-and-a-half-hour climb from the nearest road.

Martin made model airplanes out of split bamboo to thrust off the peak of his parents' roof and see how far they'd soar. He eventually even built one with a tiny engine. As the years went by, he got himself into aviation ground school while he was still a high school student at Faith Academy in Manila. By the time he graduated in 1977, his goal was firm: to go home to America, buy a car, become a pilot, and make lots of money.

But then his dad said, "Wait a minute, Martin. We want you to do at least one year of Bible school." Martin wasn't happy about that at all, thinking it would just delay him from what he really wanted to do: fly.

A spirited debate raged, but in the end, he submitted to his parents' wishes and trekked to New Tribes Bible Institute in Jackson, Michigan. He did his classwork, even though he says he was "cold all the time!" He'd grown up in the tropics where you wear shorts and a T-shirt, or maybe a pair of jeans at the most. Even shoes were optional in much of the Philippines. Martin refused to dress warmly at school, and he said the Michigan winter just about froze him to death.

Nevertheless, it was during that year that the first small spark of a future in missions was kindled for Martin. As he studied the

Scriptures, he thought back to the mission pilots he'd known in the Philippines and mulled the possibility of joining their ranks after all.

The next summer, he moved (with his parents' blessing) back to Wichita, the "air capital of the world." In Wichita, Martin got his flight training and his Airframe and Powerplant certificate, a license that allowed him to work on aircraft. His uncle Ron Eyres got him a job at Coleman, the camping-equipment manufacturer, and helped him find an apartment in an elderly lady's basement.

It wasn't long before his night-school air mechanics instructor saw Martin's potential and recommended him for a job on the flight line at Cessna Aircraft. That allowed him to join the Cessna Flying Club, which opened up all kinds of opportunities to fly.

One day, Martin received the news that a New Tribes Mission pilot he knew well in the Philippines had crashed his plane and been killed. Martin could well envision the gap in service that would leave. Who would step in to fill it? Maybe the Lord wanted him to complete his Bible studies after all.

Rose Hill Bible Church, which his family had helped start, was without a pastor at that point, and a professor from Calvary Bible College was filling in. Martin volunteered to fly up to Kansas City each Saturday and pick him up, then return him the following evening. That gave him a lot of time to talk to the man about the college's program and the whole idea of Christian service.

One thing led to another, and soon Calvary's missionary aviation program contacted him to say, "If you'll come as a student, you can teach a course or two in our flight department." And that's how this wonderful young man showed up in my life.

• • •

One day in the summer of 1982 Martin told me, "My sister just graduated from Faith Academy, and my mom is bringing her back to the States to get ready for college. They're flying in here; would you like to come with Doug and me to the airport?"

"Sure," I said, excited to learn more about what this family was like.

When they came out of the Jetway, we saw that there were three of them: Cheryl, Martin's mother, and little Felicia. I could tell that Martin's mother was not entirely happy with him for bringing me along—after all, I wasn't even a family member and I was taking up space that could have been used for luggage! We wound up holding suitcases on our laps.

But as the minutes ticked by, we all got along fine. We stopped at a pancake house to eat, and I sat there amused and amazed as I listened to this very practical family make plans. It was almost like a business meeting: "Okay, we are going to do this, and then this and this, and do you need anything for this . . . ?" I was watching a family that was used to living apart from one another, so they just dived right in to the necessary logistics, while Felicia played contentedly with the little coffee creamers, drinking them down one by one.

In a few weeks, Oreta and Felicia returned to the Philippines. I still wasn't sure where I stood with Martin's mom. When I asked him, however, he said, "You did just fine. She thinks you're really nice."

As Martin and I continued to date, I became more and more convinced that this was indeed a very special man. I was definitely falling in love—no question about it. And I could tell that he loved me, too.

I had planned to go home to visit my parents over spring break in 1983, and Martin decided to go with me. "Let's take off early and meet about noon," he suggested. "We can be all ready to start driving then, and that way we won't arrive in Arkansas at an unearthly hour."

I left work early, but when I arrived at the appointed place, Martin wasn't ready yet. I thought, *This is kind of odd. He told me to be ready, and he's not.* It was out of character for him.

Finally he showed up, a bit breathless. He apologized for being late, and we headed out of the city. By late afternoon we had traveled as far as Springfield, Missouri, where we stopped to eat at the Battlefield Mall McDonald's. As we sat together in the booth, we had so much fun goofing around and laughing. I was talking very animatedly when the ketchup in my hand squirted all over my shirt. We laughed and laughed. I just kind of wiped it off with a napkin, and soon it was time to go.

"Aren't you going to clean up your shirt?" Martin asked.

"Well, no, I hadn't really planned on it. We'll be home in a few hours, and I'll change then."

He got an odd look on his face and said, "You know, I really feel like you ought to wash your shirt."

I didn't say anything, but I was a little irritated. *You were the one who was late—and now you're telling me to go waste more time washing off my shirt?* I thought.

I went into the rest room, squirted soap from the dispenser onto the red stain, scrubbed it off, and stood under the blow-dryer for a few minutes. I went back out. "Is this better?" I asked him.

"Yeah, I think it's really good that you did that."

We drove another hour or so, until we saw a sign ahead that pointed right: "Burnham 2 miles."

Martin slowed down and looked at the sign. "Have you ever been to Burnham, Missouri?" he asked me.

"Well, to tell you the truth, yes—one time I was on my way home and pulled off to see it. There's nothing there."

"Well, I think I want to see it," he said. He turned up the gravel road toward the few buildings that still remained: an old, dilapidated filling station that had gone out of business, a Burnham Baptist Church, and maybe one or two houses.

"Hey, let's get out and check the service times at this church," he said brightly.

Oh brother, I thought. *Now we're really wasting time. I thought the whole point was to get to Arkansas at a decent hour!*

But I didn't say anything. We got out and walked over to the steep-roofed building with brown siding. And then . . . he pulled a tiny ring box from his pocket.

"Gracia . . . would you marry me?"

I gasped. So that was what this detour had been all about! I looked up into his face in shock and said, "Are you sure?!"

"Yeah, I'm sure!" Martin said with a grin.

"Are you *sure* you're sure?"

"I'm sure."

I was getting up the courage to say yes, but in that moment, a flock of worries crowded into my mind. I wondered if I should wait to talk to my folks about such a big decision. But I knew I had absolutely no doubts about marrying Martin. And I knew my parents approved of this relationship. In fact, Martin was already popular with my dad, who had flown in World War II in Italy. When he had heard I was dating a pilot, he was enthusiastic. The fact that Martin was an MK made it even better.

"I've already talked to your dad, and he says it's fine," Martin's voice broke into my thoughts. I quickly snapped back to reality.

"Yes, I'll marry you!" I cried. We fell into a long hug right there on the front lawn of the Burnham Baptist Church.

He ran back to the car to get his camera. Now everything started making sense—why he wanted me to deal with the ketchup on my shirt, and why he had been late that morning. He'd been running around the campus making sure he had everything ready to make this day perfect.

We talked and laughed the rest of the trip. He told me he had already had a "she's the one!" phone conversation with his parents back in the Philippines, and they had assured him they would come for a wedding that summer even though it wasn't time for their next furlough.

When we arrived at my parents' home around seven o'clock, supper was waiting in the Crock-Pot. What a special celebration we enjoyed together as my family gazed at my ring and congratulated us.

• • •

We were married in Kansas City on May 28, 1983, just a few short months after we had gotten engaged. The ceremony and reception were simple but meaningful as we celebrated our happiness with friends and family.

We spent our honeymoon in Branson, Missouri, long before it was the famous tourist destination it is today. We had so much fun and made so many wonderful memories, I just knew my life was going to be wonderful as long as Martin was by my side.

All too soon, it was time to leave. At the end of that week, we were due in the far southwestern corner of Nebraska, where Martin had landed a summer job as a crop duster with Stegg's Flying Service. We made quick stops in Arkansas and then in Rose Hill to say good-bye to Martin's parents, who were soon returning to the Philippines.

In the farm town of Imperial, Nebraska, we settled into a little apartment and quickly began to make friends. We attended Imperial Bible Church, and everyone was so kind to us; newlyweds sort of bring out the hospitality in people, I suppose. We were often invited places for a meal or a dessert, and I got involved in a women's Bible study. I took a class on refinishing furniture so we could redo some antique chairs my mom and dad had given us. It was a wonderful summer.

Before long, Martin was offered a permanent job by one of the farmers there. We talked about it at length. "You know, it would be so easy to settle down in this community and make a good living, wouldn't it?" Martin said one evening, staring out at the big Western sky. The money was indeed attractive. "But that's not what we're called to do."

He was right. Even though we really loved it there, we both felt that God had other plans for us. So we decided that we'd better leave Imperial before we got too rooted. We headed back to Calvary Bible College that fall so Martin could teach again in the aviation department until the next New Tribes Mission orientation cycle came around.

4
ROOKIES
(1984–87)

NEW TRIBES CALLED IT "boot camp"—a year of primitive living and demanding study so they could determine if you were cut out for foreign service or if you just thought you were. Martin and I landed in the small Southern town of Durant, Mississippi, one January day in 1984 and moved into a one-room apartment in a converted Civil War hospital. Our apartment had a stove and a refrigerator, but the common bathroom was down the hall. We had to carry our water from the bathroom back into our apartment in order to do the dishes and then carry our slop water up the hill and pour it into a pit when we were finished.

We were required to haul our garbage to another special pit up the hill. Everything in this compound was meant to imitate the way we might be called upon to live overseas. The mission wanted everyone to have both eyes open about the realities of tribal ministry.

Our boot-camp group included three families with kids, two other couples, and two single women. The living conditions were pretty rough, and it was no wonder that we bonded very closely with the others in our group. We also made some really good friends at the First Presbyterian Church in nearby Kosciusko. Those people welcomed us warmly.

Our weekday classes during boot camp covered everything

from ecclesiology to sociology. We spent a lot of time study-
ing what a New Testament church really is—not necessarily an
American church, but the essentials of the church God wants to
be established regardless of context. We did cross-cultural work,
taking up an extended case study of the Yurok Indians in northern
California, their traditions, their values, and their god, *Wapakumu*.
We pretended we were Yuroks, and each person in the group had
to attempt to teach a lesson that would make sense, with fitting
illustrations. For example, if portraying Jesus as "the Lamb of God"
would only mystify the Yuroks, we needed to come up with a way
to solve the dilemma. It was an excellent education.

As far as finances were concerned, once again, things were
pretty simple. New Tribes Mission is not a cushy operation. All
missionaries and would-be missionaries are required to raise their
own funds. The head office in Sanford, Florida, serves as a collec-
tion point for receipting purposes but makes no guarantees and
provides no safety net. Whatever dollars come in are forwarded to
the missionaries—no processing fees deducted, but no extra grants
added either. If their account plunges in a particular month, the
problem is theirs alone.

After several months, Martin's parents began to send about
fifty dollars a month, even though they had their own missionary
budget to worry about. Several of our college friends began sending a little as well, and soon our monthly total came to somewhere
near one hundred dollars. We mainly lived off our savings from the
summer of crop dusting in Imperial. Needless to say, we watched
every penny.

I can't say that Martin and I loved boot camp. After all, we both
had college degrees and felt like we knew a few things. Here, we
were simply a couple of rookies; it was kind of a blow to our pride.
But it was a necessary experience.

We learned to get along with people who weren't like us, we
learned to live in close quarters, and we learned to obey leadership, even when we didn't agree with their decisions. We figured

out ways to be hospitable on a shoestring budget, because even if we didn't have a lot of money or food, we were still put on the rotation schedule to host visitors when they came through. It was great training for what happens all the time on the mission field.

Our training included "jungle camp," a period of time when we were dispatched to go live in the woods. We had to build a house from only what we could carry to the site. When our time for jungle camp arrived, Martin constructed a quite respectable A-frame in the middle of the woods—the first home we ever owned! Then several days later, he returned for me. We packed up everything we would need for six weeks and rafted across the lake to our spot.

We carried all our food, because we knew we weren't allowed to go out for anything. If we had forgotten something important, we would just have had to live without it. After a hard morning of lugging the gear and supplies up the hill, Martin set up the half barrel he had cut to make a stove so I could cook over a wood fire. It even had an oven that worked very well.

Although jungle camp was pretty rough, it truly was a special time for Martin and me, as well as those training with us. I have special memories of the guys kneading bread and baking it over hot coals. We celebrated our first anniversary there and enjoyed the top tier of our wedding cake. (When you're young and in love, you remember to bring along those important items!)

We made our own fun. Many a night we played Dutch Blitz and Trivial Pursuit long into the night.

Near the end of that six weeks, Martin had to leave for pilot evaluation at the mission's flight base in Arizona. That didn't win me any reprieve from jungle camp; I was expected to fend for myself. I was thrilled when my parents made a special trip to visit me in my little jungle home. I even managed to fix them a halfway decent meal.

I was doing okay all alone—until suddenly the announcement came one morning: "Today you're all moving back home. Pack up."

This was part of the training strategy, to throw us curveballs and see how we adjusted.

"But I have no husband to help me pack up," I protested.

"Yes, you're right. But that may happen to you on the mission field someday," our leader replied.

I had no choice but to get our stuff together and carry it all down the hill to the lake, where a teenager helped me raft it across. I loaded it onto the tractor-trailer for the return to the compound, grumbling under my breath the entire time about what a dirty deal this was.

When I finally finished hauling our belongings back up the two flights of stairs to our little apartment, I was dripping wet with sweat. I decided to head for the backyard swimming pool. *I deserve a pity party!* I told myself.

At the pool I met a woman whose family was passing through on furlough. I began complaining to her about how upset I was at having to move home from jungle camp without my husband to help.

She listened quietly, then said, "Would you like to hear what just happened to me?" She went on to explain that her husband had just had a heart attack in the jungle overseas. He had been flown out of their village and then immediately evacuated to the States for medical care. This woman had been left alone to pack up her entire house all by herself and move out—with several young children.

I was duly rebuked. *So this is what boot camp is for,* I thought, *to find out if we can handle adversity and take what life sends our way.* I learned so much during those days. I learned that sometimes we need to go through a lot of unpleasantness in order to get the job done. That life isn't always wonderful. That happiness is not dependent on our circumstances but on our attitudes. Little did I know how important those lessons would be sixteen years later in the Philippine rain forest.

• • •

When we left boot camp after a year, I was devastated. We had bonded with these eighteen people, and it tore my heart out to say good-bye. I cried and carried on until I realized, *Girl, your whole life is going to be a series of good-byes. You've got to get your act together if you're going to survive in the future.* I determined never again to let good-byes devastate me as they had this time.

We had been certified to move to the next level of missionary training, which took us to the flight base in Arizona. There Martin's work involved more intensive preparation for the technical side of mission work.

When discussions began about where we would actually serve, Martin went to the leadership and said, "Please send us anywhere except the Philippines." Not that he disliked the country—but he had grown up there and was worried about acceptance as an adult. Would the old-timers in the mission, who remembered him as a little kid, be willing to crawl into an airplane and entrust their lives to him now? Maybe it would be better to go somewhere else.

I personally didn't care where we went. Martin was so fun to live with and I was so in love with him that I knew I'd be happy anywhere as long as we were together.

The leaders understood Martin's concerns and began to talk about the needs in Paraguay. This went on for a while, and we were feeling pretty positive about this option. But then one day, we were called in for another meeting.

"You know, they really do need a replacement pilot in the Philippines," we were told. "Martin, you know the culture and you partly know the language. It's kind of ridiculous to send you somewhere else. Would you be willing to go back?"

Without hesitation, Martin nodded yes. He was just that kind of person. Wherever he was asked to serve, he would accept the call willingly.

Because of his prior language exposure, they waived our

requirement of language prep school. The need on the field was urgent, they said, so we were given a quick target date for arrival: early 1986. We still didn't have any financial support to speak of, and our crop-duster savings were basically gone. Obviously, we would have to get busy on the fund-raising front.

This was tough for Martin. "Gracia, I just don't like the idea of begging for money from strangers," he told me. "We're not that kind of people."

"I know," I agreed. "What if we just talk to people who know us, the ones who have already shown interest in us? Would that be enough to take care of our needs?"

We didn't know but decided it was worth a try. We began by calling Jack Middleton, the pastor of Wichita Bible Church, where Martin had attended.

"We're headed for the mission field," Martin announced cheerfully that autumn day. "We are going to go early next year."

"Sure you are!" Jack said with a hearty laugh. "Don't you know how long it takes a missionary to raise support these days? Three years! And you're going to do it in less than three months?"

"Well, they really need us in the Philippines," Martin replied, unflustered. "If we get the cash for the tickets, we're going to go. We'll figure out the monthly support later." That was just how Martin thought. He had seen the Lord supply for his family time and again while growing up in the Philippines, so he didn't feel it was presumption on his part to make such a statement now. In his heart, he just knew. Martin's confidence and faith in God were so strong, they were contagious. I had no worries or concerns.

We didn't hear from Jack after that, so we made other contacts. Back in Mississippi, the young-couples Sunday school class that Martin had taught got inspired to help. "We are going to try to take care of your tickets to get to the field," they said when they called us. (Those tickets cost around two thousand dollars.) "You pray for us—we've never done anything like this before. But we're going to have some spaghetti suppers and garage sales, and see what we can do."

A week later, they called back with even more exuberance. "We not only have money for your tickets, but we have enough money for you to ship your stuff!"

Whoa—it was clear our pledge was being kicked into gear, ready or not. We thanked them profusely, and as soon as the money arrived, we took a deep breath and purchased our tickets for February.

When Pastor Middleton heard what was happening, he called an emergency meeting of his church's missions committee about a week before we left. He asked us to make a special appearance to explain our vision.

When we finished, they said, "Hey, we really want to support you. We just thought we had plenty of time to make our decision." By the end of the evening, they had put themselves on the line for a monthly sum. We thanked them and went back to packing.

We found that, generally, as soon as people knew we had our tickets and were really going, our support picked up. When we got to the field, it picked up even more, and we always had what we needed. I'm not advocating this approach for anyone else. I'm sure there are other valid ways to fund missionary work. But this is the way God chose to work for us.

We were set to leave for the Philippines on the very day that President Ferdinand Marcos had to flee the country. The Filipino people decided they'd had enough of dictatorial rule and came out in droves to overthrow him. Because of the unrest, our travel agent called to say our flight had been canceled but rescheduled for two weeks later. Here we were, "all dressed up and no place to go."

We passed the two weeks enjoying more time with relatives, and soon enough, the day of departure arrived again. A small group gathered at the Wichita airport—my parents, various relatives, friends from local churches. I must say that I handled good-byes very well that day. In my mind I pretended that I'd see these folks again the following week, so I didn't need to indulge in tears or drama.

But when we got on the Philippine Airlines flight at Los Angeles International Airport, the greetings to the passengers began in Tagalog instead of English. Suddenly tears began streaming down my face. I was truly leaving home, and I didn't know when or if I would ever return. But then Martin held my hand, and I didn't cry long.

When we stepped off the plane in Manila, the humidity nearly took my breath away. Walking into the terminal reminded me of times I had spent in the jungle house at the Wichita zoo—it was humid and very warm. Steve Roberts, New Tribes Mission's chief mechanic, picked us up, and as we wove through traffic, there seemed to be no rules. The lines painted on the pavement meant nothing. I was thinking how brave this man was when, all of a sudden, a little kid walked out into five lanes of traffic and right in front of our car. I almost sucked my teeth down my throat. The little guy was just trying to sell newspapers!

After that drive, our New Tribes Mission guesthouse was a welcome haven. When we went to bed that night, I was totally wiped out. But about three-thirty in the morning, my eyes popped open— my first experience with jet lag.

As I lay there, I listened to the night noises in Manila. What was that I heard—roosters? *Why are there roosters in a city?* I wondered. Martin woke up soon afterward and explained to me that roosters are everywhere in the Philippines, not just on farms.

The next morning, it was time to get busy. We sat down with the business manager for some orientation. Charlie Breithaupt pulled out the agenda sheet and said something like, "Okay, mailboxes— well, Martin, you've been here before so you know how the mail system works. . . . Finances—you've been here before; you know how that works."

I sat there hoping Martin had a good memory, because I was clueless.

Martin said, "Well, actually, I left here when I was just out of high school. You'd better back up and treat us like any other new couple."

For the next couple of days we went through all the necessary orientation. They took us to get our Philippine driver's licenses; we also had to stop at Immigration to be fingerprinted. But soon we were on our way north into the interior of Luzon Island, a seven-hour bus ride to a mission compound with an airstrip at Aritao.

The compound was located in a beautiful area. Our home was built up off the ground on stilts. We even had a bathroom inside the house and running cold water. Out on the veranda was a porch swing, my absolute favorite thing about the house. I knew it would be a wonderful place to sit and enjoy the beauty of the mountains and to watch the farmers plowing with their water buffalo in the rice fields down in the valley.

Very few missionaries live in communities like the one at Aritao anymore. It's rare to find groups of houses all clustered together like that, but it was standard practice back in the 1950s when this one was built. Such a design can certainly be questioned for its "us-them" appearance. However, it does have some practical advantages. The missionary staff certainly communicates better since everyone's so close. They also avoid sickness better because they're living in a more controlled environment.

New Tribes Mission had three airplanes in the Philippines: a Super Cub, a Helio Courier, and a Cessna. The plane Martin began flying right away was a red-and-white Helio Courier. He was in the air almost immediately, tending to the needs of missionary families who worked with four different remote tribes on Luzon. He delivered everything from milk powder to eggs, meat, and fuel for refrigerators and stoves.

I had hardly had time to unpack in our little two-bedroom house before I took over the radio responsibilities. Twice a day—once at 7:00 A.M. and again at 3:30 P.M.—I went through roll call and talked with each tribal station. If anyone had "traffic," as we called it, meaning messages for anyone else, I made a list and then started matching up the parties like an old-time telephone operator. I also took grocery orders, medicine orders, requests for appointments, and flight needs.

I had never done anything like this before, but in a way it reminded me of my old days at Calvary Bible College, when I had had four bosses. I would be up to my ears in producing some document, and the president would walk by and say, "Oh, I have a chapel announcement—take this down . . . ," and instantly I'd have to stop whatever I was doing and begin typing what he said. The phone would be ringing, and people would be coming in to see the chaplain or the dean—I was used to multitasking, I guess. I could tell already that's how this flight program was going to be.

The other part of radio work was to "flight-follow" Martin whenever he was in the air. He called me every ten minutes or so with a position report, which I recorded in case of an emergency, so I'd know his last location. I also had to keep track of the weather by checking with the person at the destination. In other words, whenever he was in the air, I sat by the radio and never left.

To be quite honest, I loved it all. I settled right into it. We were instantly busy, and that's what we wanted.

A friend of ours on the field once wrote a humorous letter to his financial supporters that we found gratifying. He said that if you ask a group of missionary kids, "What's the grossest thing you've ever had to eat?" you will get all kinds of different answers, depending on the country where they've grown up. An MK from the Philippines will say one thing, somebody from Bolivia will say something else, somebody from the Congo something else.

But if you follow up with the question, "So how did you get it down the hatch?" the kids will all give you the same answer: ketchup!

And how do missionary kids and their families in remote areas stay well stocked on this vital substance called ketchup? Answer: the missionary pilot! Without his assistance, everyone would be in big trouble.

Martin's initial fears that his flying ability would not be given full credit in the Philippines proved somewhat true at first, but people quickly were won over by his exceptional abilities as time and time again he put the Cessna down safely on airstrips as short as three hundred meters with trees crowding in on both sides. His skill was little short of amazing. He could stop a fully loaded plane on a dime, and sometimes he needed to do just that. I admit I'm an admiring wife saying this, but it really was true. And after he hopped out of the cockpit, people quickly realized how big a heart he had for tribal people and for the frontline missionaries trying to serve them. He knew that people who hadn't talked to another English speaker in weeks just needed someone to hold a cup of coffee and listen.

Before long, Martin knew everything about every missionary. He knew who was struggling financially. He knew which husbands and wives weren't getting along. He knew who was discouraged with language study because they weren't catching on as fast as they had hoped. He saw the newborn babies. He got to congratulate MKs on their homeschool projects. He met villagers who had recently become believers.

Martin was the perfect person to hear it all. He just had a heart for everyone he came in contact with, and everyone who knew him loved him.

As for our own financial situation, we saw the Lord provide for us in amazing ways. Yes, there were times when we didn't eat very well; there were times when we walked instead of taking Martin's motorcycle. But we always had what we truly needed.

• • •

We had been at Aritao about six months when I gave Martin some very happy news one day: We were going to have a baby!

When I approached my due date in February 1987, Martin flew me to Manila, which had the closest hospital with a proper maternity department. We stayed at the mission guesthouse while we waited for the baby to arrive.

Martin was supposed to leave for a safety seminar in New Guinea, and the baby wasn't here yet. Obviously, he didn't want to be gone for the big event. My due date came and went.

A couple of days later, the Filipino doctor finally said, "You are starting to dilate. We'll go ahead and admit you, and we'll just induce labor and get this over with." But although they gave me the drugs to induce labor, the baby still didn't come and didn't come. It was a long and painful day and we were all starting to get a little nervous.

After many hours, the doctor came in again, looked at me, and said, "We are going to help you."

I didn't quite know what he meant, but I soon found out. I was wheeled into the delivery room, and before I realized what was happening, two interns stepped up on either side of me— and basically pushed Jeffrey into the world! I had never had any Lamaze classes, but I'd done some reading about giving birth, and I remember thinking to myself, *I don't think this is how you're supposed to do it!*

Thankfully, Jeffrey was fine and so was I. In fact, I felt so good we were ready to leave in less than twenty-four hours. Martin signed all the papers, paid our bill (I think it was around seventy-five dollars), and it was time to go.

"Where are my clothes to go home in?" I asked when he came to get me.

"Oops, I forgot them," Martin replied. "Can't you just wear what you have on?"

That wasn't exactly what I had in mind, especially in front of all the wealthy people who patronized this prominent hospital. But there wasn't much choice. I ended up being wheeled out the front door in my bathrobe.

Of course, we didn't have a vehicle in Manila, so we had to use a taxi. Martin went out to the street and waved down an old rickety taxi. The car had no air conditioner and was about to fall apart, but the driver was so proud on the thirty-minute drive to the guesthouse because he was taking an American home with his firstborn son! Martin gave him a big tip.

Oreta, Martin's mother, came to Manila for the arrival of her first grandchild. Martin had to leave for New Guinea, but Oreta stayed and continued to take care of me while he was gone. She and I bonded more closely than ever during those days in the guesthouse; she served me wonderfully and taught me what to do with a newborn.

It wasn't long, however, before we were back home in Aritao, a family of three. We could not have been happier.

5
TODDLERS AND TRAFFIC

(1987–2000)

JEFF WAS STILL A TINY BABY when a delegation of New Tribes missionaries from the southern island of Mindanao came to see us one day.

"We really, really need a flight program on our island," they said. "There are eight families altogether—more than you have here on Luzon. Would you consider coming down and putting something together?"

Martin flew down to check out the prospects. He found, as we had been told, a place of rich natural resources but less development on this, the second largest island of the Philippines. It was a long way from the bustle and advantages of Manila. It was also closer to the Muslim minority population, which for decades had resented living under "Christian" domination, as they viewed it.

But the needs for aviation support were obvious. We began working toward a move, lining up a replacement for our present post, and rebuilding an airplane, a Piper Super Cub, for this new post. I helped out every chance I got, usually when Jeff was sleeping. The Super Cub's surfaces are fabric rather than metal, and I enjoyed sewing the fabric onto the struts along with the other NTM missionaries. This kind of sewing is a two-person job, one on each side of the wing, so we had plenty of opportunity for talking and joking.

Soon we packed up and headed for Malaybalay ["m'*lye*-b'*lye*"], a small city in the mountains with several colleges. Martin found a home for his airplane almost sooner than he found a home for us; the municipal airport leased him space to build a hangar there, and construction started right away. Meanwhile, we stayed at the mission's guesthouse while we house hunted. There was no mission compound here, which was fine with us; we looked forward to living in a regular neighborhood and making local friends.

One day a friend of ours saw an empty house while jogging and took Martin over to see it. He came back to me all excited. "You know, that house has real possibilities!" he said with his typical enthusiasm. "And the rent is only thirty dollars a month."

"Okay! Let's go for it!" I said without hesitation. I probably should have waited to see it first. What I found once I arrived was a place that was basically falling apart. The roof had gaping holes. And the kitchen—oh, my. Filipinos normally have what they call a "dirty kitchen" at the back of the house where they cook over an open fire. Well, in this house, the previous renters had used the house itself as their dirty kitchen, leaving the ceiling covered with soot.

"Martin! When will we ever have time to fix up this house?" I cried.

And Martin, true to form, said, "You know, I think we can do this. Don't worry."

All our coworkers said we should look elsewhere. But anything else we found was too expensive for our budget. So we began to fix up that house in our spare time. We didn't have many belongings anyway, so it's not like we had much furniture to show off. We just bought some beds and a baby bed for Jeff and moved in.

And you know, that house turned out really nice. In the back was a field where a tenant was growing peanuts, corn, and cassava. The landlord had promised us this space as soon as the current crops were harvested. So in time, we had a decent backyard. We tallied all the fruit trees one day: coconut, marang, papaya, guava, calamansi (musk lime), banana, and even some coffee trees.

Malaybalay became our home for the next eight years, and we loved everything about it. We got to know our neighbors, and even though I didn't speak much Cebuano, I went outside every afternoon when everyone sat around talking. I loved to listen to the women chat, and eventually I made some very good friendships, even though my vocabulary was limited.

On Sundays we went to Bethel Baptist Church, which had been established way back in World War II. We grew to love the people there so much. The church had an English service in addition to one in Cebuano, which was very nice for us. There were several generations of believers in Malaybalay, and we really felt a connection with these folks. They were such a fun group of people and they seemed to really like having Martin and me at their parties. This is probably because we were always willing to do something silly—like sing along with the karaoke machine or perform a goofy skit.

In late 1989, our daughter, Melinda Joy, came along. I gave birth at the nice little Baptist hospital in town, very early in the morning on October 17. A surgeon was visiting that day—they didn't have a resident staff surgeon—and the room was needed for procedures. Since I was feeling so good after the delivery, I got out of their way and went home before noon. I wanted to go and Oreta had come from Luzon to be with me, so I knew I'd receive good care.

Just for fun, I did the radio "sked" (schedule) that afternoon as if nothing had happened. I sat down at the radio, pressed the microphone button, and gave my usual opening spiel: "Good afternoon, this is 4FE202 signing on for traffic. . . ."

Diane Thomas, one of my missionary friends who knew I had just given birth, broke through on the other end. "Gracia Burnham, what are you doing on the radio?!" We had a good laugh. I hadn't missed a beat.

Mindy was a wonderful, healthy baby, but when she was only a few months old, I started not to feel well. I didn't say anything for a while, but my stomach was always upset. Finally one day I admitted to Martin, "I just don't feel good."

We thought it was probably a case of intestinal worms, a common malady in the Philippines. I took the standard worm treatment, three days' worth of Combantrin. It didn't help.

After a while, Martin said to me, "You know, Gracia, you're acting just like you did when you were pregnant with the other kids."

"Don't be ridiculous," I shot back. "I have a seven-month-old, and I'm still nursing!"

Eventually I went to the doctor for help. And would you believe it? I was pregnant again! Oh, my.

I headed out to the airport hangar to tell Martin. "It's not fair to Mindy!" I cried to him. "And it's not going to be fair to the new baby." Obviously, there wasn't anything to be done about it now, but I just had to vent. Later I consoled myself with the notion that I'd probably have another sweet little girl to play with Mindy. They could grow up together being best friends.

Well, delivery day arrived that December, a couple of weeks before Christmas—and here came Zachary, a boy with enough rambunctious energy for two babies! We took him home and loved him just as much as the first two. And even though he was unexpected, I have to say he's added a wonderful dimension to our family. The year in the jungle that I was forced to spend without him, I thought of him so often and realized just how much I would be missing if he hadn't come along to join our family.

• • •

In 1991, we finally headed home for a furlough. We had left the United States with no children. A little more than five years later, we got off the plane with three kids aged four and under. Someone gave us an old station wagon to use while we were home, and we drove all over the country visiting our list of about ten supporting churches and twenty individuals. We thanked them not only for sending checks but also for praying for us.

Our time in the States was short. In less than a year, we were back in Malaybalay, serving the eight New Tribes missionary families scattered across the island. We loved our life there. It was a wonderful time; new churches were being planted among the tribal people, and Bible translations were moving ahead at full tilt. Since these new churches were hidden up in the mountains where there were no roads, Martin stayed very busy.

I was at the radio all day, it seemed. Martin arrived at the hangar by six in the morning to load up for a flight; he preferred to fly then, when the sky tended to be clearer, before the afternoon thunderstorms built up. Meanwhile, I fed him weather information and handled anything else he needed. The flights were usually thirty to forty minutes each, plus all the miscellaneous ground time, and on some days he managed to make two round-trips instead of just one.

Things got even busier for us when the two other New Tribes pilots left the Philippine field at the same time. The Nordicks had been working on the island of Palawan but had recently lost a thirteen-month-old daughter to a mysterious, fast-moving illness. By the time they realized how seriously sick she was, she was gone. Then Sheri Nordick was diagnosed with diabetes, and right on the heels of that, their son Jake began crying day after day that his leg hurt. The Filipino doctor admitted that he didn't know what was wrong with him. "This little boy may have cancer or something," he told them. That did it—they headed almost straight for the airport to catch the next plane out for a furlough.

The other pilot and his wife had sons graduating from high school and felt they needed to be back in America with their boys. So they left as well. Suddenly Martin and I were trying to service three programs simultaneously. For a while, he went to one island and stayed two weeks, then to another island and stayed two weeks, then came back to Mindanao—this meant he was away from home for nearly a month at a time. We quickly saw that this wasn't going to work.

We asked another mission organization, Wycliffe Bible

Translators, to take over for us on Luzon, while we tried to juggle the remaining two islands. Once a month Martin made the long overwater flight to Palawan and stayed there ten days or more. Mostly he went alone, but sometimes I went along and brought the kids. The trips were tiring either way.

Palawan ["pa-*laow*-an"] is the 275-mile-long, thin island that, on a map, appears to poke out from the rest of the Philippines like a javelin thrown toward the southwest. It's a naturalist's wonder-land—a concoction of mahogany forests, stunning beaches, coral reefs, and all kinds of animals, from hornbill birds to six-foot-long monitor lizards. Near Puerto Princesa, the provincial capital, is a subterranean river you can paddle for five miles if you don't mind the bats hanging overhead. Palawan has been called "the last unspoiled frontier," although migration, logging, tourism, and pov-erty are today starting to take their toll.

For a New Tribes missionary pilot and his family, Palawan was a lonely assignment. They lived neither on a compound, like Aritao, nor in a city with other missionaries nearby, as we did in Malaybalay. They were all by themselves in a house beside the grass airstrip. They did everything, from buying supplies to keeping the books to maintaining the airplane to battling back the ever advanc-ing foliage. Because the climate was even more tropical than the rest of the Philippines, they had to think more about malaria and dengue fever. We found that every time we went to Palawan, we came home exhausted.

It helped a great deal that Martin really believed in the value of family vacations. Even though we didn't have a lot of money, he was always willing to spring for some wonderful getaways. Every year we went to Camiguin, a delightful little island that had been formed by a cluster of seven volcanoes. The only way to get there was by ferry. We'd spend a week just exploring and sitting on the white sand beach. It was so refreshing.

I always returned ready to get back to work—especially when I began to homeschool Jeff. I arranged a little desk for him right near my radio desk, so I could do both things at once if necessary. I ordered curriculum from Calvert, a well-known home-education supplier out of Maryland, and I also got some material from the missions co-op resource center on the island. As people's kids moved from grade to grade, they passed along their books and other materials to those of us with younger ones.

If a textbook didn't have a teacher's manual or a workbook, I just made up my own; after all, I'd been an education major back at Calvary. And of course, I read aloud to the kids all the time.

During Jeff's third-grade year, we took a break from home-schooling. Several of us mission families—New Tribes and Southern Baptists—got together and rented a jeepney to transport our kids each morning and afternoon to an SIL-Wycliffe school about thirty minutes away. Jeepneys are these brightly painted, colorful Philippine contraptions that look like military jeeps in the front but have benches on an extended flatbed in the back, with a metal roof overhead. They're the local version of a minivan, only they're open to the air and thus a lot more noisy.

· · ·

Early one morning, Martin was flying an American businessman and another mission colleague to the city of Davao. As usual, I was at the radio; Jeff had just gotten up and was having a bowl of cereal on the other side of a row of bookshelves we used as a partition.

Martin's voice crackled through the speaker. "Uh, Gracia, we have a problem here. . . ." Then the radio went silent.

I waited for the next word, but nothing came.

"Three-zero-nine, are you going to tell me what your problem is?" I anxiously radioed back.

"I'm losing engine power. There was a puff of smoke—I'm not sure what it was. I'm over the mountains right now and into the clouds; I'm trying to climb while I've still got power to get as much altitude as possible to work with. . . ." And then it was quiet again.

My palms began to sweat, and I prayed with all my heart. *Oh, God, help him know what to do!*

At just that moment, a Filipino friend stopped by to return a book she had borrowed. I burst out, "On your way to work, pray for Martin! Something's wrong!" She said she would.

I kept waiting for Martin's voice. Still nothing. I yelled over the partition, "Jeffrey! Are you there?"

"Yeah."

"Pray for Daddy! He's in trouble in the airplane!"

"Okay, Mom."

A few moments later I called again. "Jeff, Jeff—please pray for Daddy! He's in trouble!"

My six-year-old called back with a touch of sternness in his little voice: "Mom! I prayed already!"

The little guy had faith that he had talked to God once—and that was adequate. He had gone on eating his breakfast.

A peace seemed to settle down upon me. *Okay, God—you're going to take care of Martin, aren't you?* Some ten minutes later, Martin called again. He had gotten out of cloud cover and could see the valley in front of him. By then the engine had seized up completely and the propeller had stopped, so he was gliding with no power.

"Gracia, I'm going to head for this Wycliffe base I see, the one at Nasuli. I think I might make it."

Another four minutes of silence. I sat frozen to my chair.

Then: "Okay, I'm switching to Nasuli frequency to warn them that I'm coming. We'll be out of contact for a little bit."

Again, I held my breath.

"Gracia, we're on the ground; I made a dead-stick landing," he radioed. "There's a whole 'hallelujah meeting' going on here! Everybody is out on the runway rejoicing." He had cleared the last fence with a mere fifty feet of altitude left. The engine had pumped out all its oil through a hole in one of the lines—but my husband was safe.

I slumped down in my chair and just sat quietly for several minutes, thanking God for sparing his life.

A coworker drove to Nasuli to pick Martin up. Later as Martin walked in the gate, he glanced at his watch and said nonchalantly, "I told you I'd be back around ten, didn't I?" We just looked at each other and laughed.

• • •

Like the first one, this term of service ran longer than the standard four years, because there was no one to take Martin's place in the cockpit. Finally, in 1997 we got pilots for each island and went home again. We stayed in the States fifteen months because a plane needed to be rebuilt at the Arizona base and readied to go to the Philippines. Jeff was old enough to help in the hangar this time.

The kids were at just the right age to really enjoy traveling as we renewed contact with our supporting churches and individuals. Jeff was in sixth grade, Mindy was in third, and Zach was in second. We didn't homeschool that year; we "carschooled." Each child had a personal box of books and a little lap desk, and we did our work rolling across the highways of America. Since all three of them were together, I even figured out some joint assignments for them.

The one subject they could not work on in a bumpy car, of course, was handwriting. We had to wait for that until we stopped at a rest area or got to someone's house. But they got an education regardless. They had a little atlas in which they tracked each state we went through, putting a sticker on it. They learned a lot about the country of their roots, even though they had never really lived in the States.

For six months of that furlough we settled down in Arkansas next to my parents, and the kids went to public school. We wanted the kids to know what it was like to live in America, not just to live in a car. So we made a point of establishing a routine. Meanwhile,

Martin traveled alone to see some constituents and also made a short trip to the Philippines to take care of things.

Then the furlough was over, and the whole family returned again, this time back to our original post on Luzon at Aritao. Although the kids had made lots of friends in Arkansas, they were just as excited as we were to head "home" to the Philippines.

With other pilots in place on all three islands, Martin was named chief pilot for the Philippines. This meant he did a lot of instruction, safety management, and general oversight. He also became the substitute whenever one of the pilots had a medical problem or a family needed to go back home.

We continued to enjoy our family vacations while serving in Aritao. If we weren't at the beach, we often traveled to Baguio, the summer capital of the Philippines. Baguio is up in the mountains, so the climate is cool. We liked to rent a place there that had a kitchen, and then we'd buy our food in the local open market, where there was always a wonderful variety. We would cook vegetables I couldn't get elsewhere. Between trips to town, we'd go horseback riding or sightseeing. In the evenings, we'd enjoy a cozy fire.

By now, of course, we had a pretty good understanding of how to get along in Philippine society. For most Filipinos, bribes were just a way of life. The police stopped people for no reason at all and took their licenses on a pretense, when what they really wanted was a payoff. We always tried to tell them how wrong this was—but after all, Martin needed his driver's license, and so in the end we'd give them the money.

We had more than one ethical debate with ourselves about whether this was wrong for us to do. As the years went on, we decided the wrong was on *their* part, in stooping to extortion, rather than on our part for doing the necessary thing in response. I suppose some people would disagree with me on that, but we had clear consciences.

Our kids got an education in Philippine culture the time someone stole Zachary's bicycle. Everybody in the barrio knew who had it; in fact, we did too, because we saw the person riding it around. "Dad, that kid took my bike!" Zachary cried one day. Martin proceeded to do the logical thing—at least so far as we understood Philippine ways. He sent a go-between to talk with the parents, politely asking for our bike back.

They immediately got very upset and embarrassed, because that's not how it's done in their culture. Our go-between returned to explain that a person doesn't accuse the other person of wrongdoing. Instead, the person offers a ransom for the property, and then everyone can be happy again.

Martin said, "How about if we send you back with a homemade cake and some cookies?" We really hated to give them cash.

This was done—and they quickly returned Zachary's bike. In their view, we had established a relationship with them; we were their friends now, and they were our friends. Everyone in the barrio was pleased that we had handled this in the proper way. No one had to be ashamed or embarrassed.

The next time I had reason to think seriously about the word *ransom,* of course, a lot more than a bicycle was on the line.

6

THE PERILS OF PALAWAN

(November 2000; May 29–30, 2001)

IF YOU ASKED MY KIDS today to name a favorite memory of life in the Philippines, they'd probably say Thanksgiving Day 2000. It was one of those special occasions when we all piled into the airplane and got to fly with Martin to a tribal station.

We were on Palawan covering for the pilot who was away, and we got this great idea to surprise our missionaries there, Norm and Jacqui Rice, with a full-fledged American Thanksgiving meal. They were living in a village all alone, struggling to learn the language, and we knew this would lift their spirits.

On one of his runs into Puerto Princesa, Martin found an imported turkey. It wasn't cheap, but he brought it home anyway. We excitedly radioed Norm and Jacqui that we'd come the next day and "bring dinner."

I basically stayed up all night cooking. Besides the turkey, I made pumpkin pies and vegetables; I baked bread; I even brought along a can of cranberry sauce I'd managed to find back in Manila, which was more rare than turkey in this part of the world.

By the next morning, I had it all ready and boxed up to fly.

The approach to this particular jungle runway was about as exciting as the best roller-coaster ride at Disney World. Martin followed the tree-lined river, edging lower and lower. We all gasped as he suddenly spun off into a sharp curve at the last minute to drop onto the grass. But as always, his technique was flawless.

The Rices were in a huddle with a group of villagers at the edge of the runway. After the propeller stopped spinning, we crawled out of the plane.

"Hi, everybody! We're here! Happy Thanksgiving!"

The look on Norm's and Jacqui's faces as we started unloading our meal was unforgettable. I had a tablecloth, china, candles, and little doilies. We just kept pulling things out of boxes until we had set a beautiful table.

All the while, Norm kept teasing the kids. "So, didja bring a turkey?"

"Yeah, we did."

"Oh, you did not—you just brought a big chicken," he'd say. (That is the usual substitute for Americans in the Philippines at holiday time.)

Finally, with a great flourish, we unveiled the golden bird.

"No way, you guys! This is incredible!" They absolutely freaked out. "Where did you find this?" We told them the story as we all squealed with delight.

I'd even managed to find some Dream Whip for the dessert that day. And so, there in that little tribal hut in a Palawano village, we had a complete Thanksgiving dinner.

Afterward, we all went to the river with their dog to play in the water. Martin took the airplane back up for more landing practice. He was trying to see if, with some additional tree cutting, the approach could be less hair-raising. Late that afternoon, we flew out again. What a special memory we made that day.

• • •

It was only six months later that we were back on Palawan, this time without our children. A busy schedule of flying awaited us, so we were grateful for a chance to relax at Dos Palmas for a day.

The resort staff were right there to meet us at the commercial airport with big smiles and warm welcomes as we got off the plane. Martin and I were among thirty or so other guests who had come to Dos Palmas for a tropical getaway. Traveling on a small hotel yacht, we arrived on the island about lunchtime and had a wonderful buffet. The weather was perfect.

Two giant palm trees rose in the middle of everything—hence the name of the resort. There was a walking path around the island's perimeter for strolls or rides on rented bicycles. Other activities at the resort included diving, snorkeling, and fishing. A lovely gift shop beckoned.

Our cabin was air-conditioned and had a refrigerator. The floor was tile (this being the tropics), but the room had a nice decor. Beyond a set of drapes was the outside deck maybe three feet wide and about six feet long. I thought to myself, *This is such a perfect spot! Tomorrow morning, while Martin sleeps off his jet lag, I'll come out here and do my nails. Then maybe I'll even write some letters.* I was really looking forward to this break, even though it was to be less than twenty-four hours.

We took a nap that afternoon. I'd brought along some snacks: some pop, mozzarella sticks, and peanut M&M's for the room. We opened mail, and Martin talked nonstop about his time in the States.

Soon it was time for the evening buffet. As we were leaving the room, I said to Martin, "You know, this door doesn't look very secure."

He glanced at it and then quickly said, "No, they never do. But don't worry—I'm sure our things will be fine." After all, the resort had its own security staff patrolling the grounds.

We returned to the circular building with the thatched roof for a sumptuous spread of roast beef, fried fish, and sweet-and-sour pork. There was also a fresh salad bar—everything we could want. The open-air eating area was pleasant and breezy; dress was, of course, casual.

At the table next to us was a somewhat tall, brown-skinned man with a big smile and an attractive, young Filipina woman. Little did I anticipate that I would soon know them much better: it was Guillermo and Fe. We could tell by his accent that he was an American. When their food came, I overheard the woman say something about returning thanks for their meal. He demurred but said, "You go right ahead."

That evening, on the way back to our cabin, we noticed the videoke place. Videoke is a popular thing for Filipinos to do. Someone with a great voice was performing, and we almost stopped in to listen. But instead, we decided to keep walking and enjoy the evening air.

We stopped to overlook the pool for a while, and then we turned back toward our room. The sky was clear, the water totally still. We talked and talked late into the night, and then we went to sleep, without a care in the world.

• • •

Six hours later—and for the next year—there was neither bed nor hot water nor electricity nor Bible, not even the most basic things of a woman's life. I woke up each day with nothing to accomplish— nothing at all, except to stay alive. What a strange feeling this was, compared to my previous life as a busy missionary wife, mother of three growing children, homeschooling teacher, family bookkeeper, letter writer, household organizer, flight supporter at the radio, hostess to a never-ending stream of houseguests—my "to do" list had constantly overflowed. Now, the page was entirely blank.

The first days aboard the fishing boat, I didn't even have to belabor what to wear. There was no choice: it would be the same gray short-sleeved shirt I had worn round the clock since the abduction.

Sonny, the Dos Palmas cook, at least had a little dirty kitchen with a woodstove to use in preparing meals for us all. He used fish brought up from the hold below; there was also a stash of rice. One night they gave us something hot to drink—coffee, we assumed. It actually tasted quite good. The truth was it had been prepared from rice that had been burned all the way to a charcoal state, then mixed with water.

Guillermo volunteered to become our "water boy," perching on the edge of the boat with a pail to bring up water for washing. (Not that I could get very clean with salt water—I learned that soap won't lather up at all—but at least it was better than nothing.) This task sounds easy, except that with the boat moving along at a good speed, Guillermo had to be very careful not to get pulled overboard.

Our freshwater came from two large plastic barrels, perhaps fifty gallons each in capacity. The longer we traveled, however, the more we were warned to conserve. Rizza, however, seemed not to get the picture; more than once I noticed her washing out her clothes, probably in order to keep looking her best for Reggie. "Oh, Rizza, please don't use up our water!" I begged. My pleas didn't do much good.

Rizza didn't seem to get the whole idea of Muslim modesty, either. The Abu Sayyaf admonished her at least to wear a long-sleeved shirt, which she did—but then promptly unbuttoned the front down low.

Eventually, we could tell that the freshwater was running low, as "floaties" started to appear. Soon it was completely gone and we were forced to resort to drinking melted ice brought up from the fish hold below. Yes, the smell and taste were less than appetizing.

Guillermo was another one who never quite bought into the modesty idea. Muslim men are supposed to be covered at all times from the navel to below the knees. Somehow that didn't stop Guillermo from stripping down to his Skivvies in order to take a saltwater bath (or more precisely, to pour water from a dipper over his head). Everybody else on the boat was just dying with embarrassment, especially the Abu Sayyaf.

"Martin, come on!" he called out. "Join me for a bath."

"No, no, that's all right. You go ahead."

All of this did not endear Guillermo to the captors. They had pretty well tagged him as a "bad guy." Martin, on the other hand, was viewed as a "good man" (even though he was a Christian missionary) because he didn't drink, didn't smoke, didn't swear, and he had a wife and children.

Our captors raised their eyebrows, though, when they went through Martin's wallet and came across a picture of Felicia, Martin's sister in her midtwenties, who is beautiful, with long blonde hair. "Who is this?!" they demanded, assuming she was Martin's girlfriend.

"Oh, that's my little sister," he replied. This seemed to settle their concerns.

Several of the younger Abu Sayyaf began to figure out that Martin was handy with mechanical things. Soon they had him fixing their transistor radios and showing them how to set the watches they had stolen. They had been randomly pushing buttons and getting nowhere up to that point. He also gave lessons on how to use their newly acquired cameras.

They began sorting out the ID materials they had swept out of our rooms, and in fact, returned many of them. They never gave back Martin's pilot licenses, though. He had worked his way through layers of Philippine bureaucracy to get those little slips of paper, and now they were gone. (At a later point, we happened to notice a bag in the wheelhouse, and when we peeked inside, it was the leftover documents. We promptly snuck these out, keeping some things, including a 2001 pocket calendar, and shredding others into the ocean.)

• • •

A sober, moon-faced captor named Musab established himself as the Abu Sayyaf's spiritual leader and began conducting Koran studies up in the bow of the boat. Those who attended were soon bored to death with his lengthy orations.

They had Korans, but only two in the whole group had read the book all the way through. One day, after listening to them read in a distinctly nasal, singsong tone, Martin asked one of the guys, "What did that say?"

"Oh, we don't know," he responded. "We just learned how to pronounce the words in Arabic, but we don't know what they mean."

"Really?"

"Of course not. We don't know Arabic."

I asked, "Why don't you translate the Koran into Tagalog, then, so you know what you're reading?"

"Oh, no, no—then it would be corrupted. The only true Koran is in Arabic."

Our captors, however, seemed eager to show us the similarities between Christianity and Islam. In fact, we do share a number of the same personages, such as Adam, Abraham, Moses, and David—they termed them all "prophets." When they found out that our youngest son was named Zachary, their faces lit up: "Oh yes, Zacarias!" they said, and congratulated us for naming our child for one of their prophets. They even began calling Martin by the name "Abu Zacarias" (father of Zachary).

One of the captors was named Zacarias as well—the short, stocky one who had ransacked our room. He had a unique personality and really liked to make people laugh, especially with his fractured English. Sometimes he excitedly combined phrases into fanciful sayings, like, when it started to rain, "The rain is coming and the people are running!" Everybody just stared at him and then cracked up.

On Tuesday afternoon, our third day in captivity, the sat-phone batteries went dead. This greatly upset Sabaya and the others. How would they keep making their pronouncements to the outside world? Soon Martin and Chito came to their rescue by showing them how to line up six D-cell batteries and pack them together securely enough to recharge the sat-phone battery.

"You know, you guys really ought to think about getting a solar panel," Martin suggested. "That way you wouldn't be so dependent on these batteries that run down." They thought that was a great idea and promptly called one of their buddies on land to order one.

Watching all this, I said to Martin, "Maybe you ought to keep your bright ideas to yourself, you know? You're going to become so indispensable to this group they'll never let us go!" On the other hand, it was to our advantage for them to continue communicating. So maybe Martin's advice served our purposes after all.

Somewhere along the line—perhaps in appreciation?—they finally got Martin a white T-shirt with sleeves, so he wouldn't be so cold at night. I tried to help out by sharing part of my *malong* with him.

One other provision came along: a few toothbrushes for the group. Martin and I were glad to get one to share between us. It was our only possession besides the clothes on our backs. No toothpaste, however.

Letty, the Chinese-Filipino businesswoman, was a middle-aged person of means. I could tell she was very worried for the safety of her young daughter and niece; she almost never took her eyes off them.

She moved over by me one afternoon with a second concern. "I've started my monthly period," she whispered, self-consciousness written all over her face. "What am I going to do?!"

I looked around the boat in vain. "Uh . . . I don't know what to tell you," I replied, hopelessly. I walked around a bit, trying to think what I would do if it were me.

Then I came up with an idea—a bad one, to be sure. But at this point, I was scavenging for any option. "Over there on the floor of the engine room, there's some cardboard. Maybe we could soften it up somehow if we cut it up in pieces and played with it awhile. . . ."

"Oh, no, no, that won't work," she said, and went off to search the boat.

Not too many minutes later she came back with cardboard in her hand and began to rip it up quietly. The rest of us ladies silently joined in the effort, kneading it with our hands to smooth out the rough edges.

(I don't know why I didn't think to mention Rizza's stash of extra clothes! That would have been a much better answer.)

Pretty soon a little knot of girls began to laugh uproariously at something. What in the world could be funny? I went over to check them out, and they were dreaming up commercials for this new kind of feminine hygiene product—ideas on how to package it, how to advertise, sales slogans to use—it was hilarious. As I watched these girls giggling, I thought to myself, *Isn't it amazing how the human mind can find humor in even the darkest situations?*

Sssssst! Sssssst! Sssssst! The Abu Sayyaf began to hiss at us, using the typical Philippine sound that means "Cut it out! Shut up!" Too much humor was not appropriate in a climate of jihad. But our funny bones were all thoroughly tickled by then and we couldn't calm down regardless of their scolding. Eventually, we asked Solaiman if we could start making a list of things we needed, not just Letty, but all the women. He agreed and gave us a piece of paper.

Now most people in this situation would probably stick to the basics: soap, shampoo, etc. But oh no—our list looked like we were headed to some kind of mall: Sunsilk for oily hair, Rejoice shampoo with conditioner, Secret solid deodorant, Colgate toothpaste, Close-Up minty fresh toothpaste, Dial soap, various pieces of underwear by size—it was crazy! I sat there chuckling to myself and thinking, *Shouldn't we be just a little more realistic here?*

Finally someone turned to me and said, "What do you want?"

"Any kind of soap would be good," I replied, "and I think we ought to have a box of amoxicillin." With sixty of us on this boat built for only ten fishermen, I knew it was just a matter of time before someone got sick.

They then took this long list, which included everything from cologne to bras, to Sabaya. He gave it one glance and handed it back, saying, "Well, figure up how much all this is going to cost."

Janice took charge of the accounting effort. The estimate came to some 14,000 pesos ($280).

Back to Sabaya again. "Well, you don't have that much," he announced. "Of the money we took from your rooms, you get 10 percent, which is only 2,000 pesos. Go back and cut it down." Faces fell all around as we headed back to try to write a more down-to-earth shopping list.

When that effort was finished, a messenger was sent on a speedboat to head for shore and bring back supplies. He left but never returned. We heard later on the radio that he was spotted in town by the authorities and arrested. We also wondered if perhaps he had defected. Anyway, we got nothing from our list!

●   ●   ●

The hardest part of those early days on the boat, of course, was every time my thoughts turned to Jeff and Mindy and Zach. We knew that the mission policy was to evacuate our kids out of the country so as not to leave opportunity for further mischief. But we kept wondering who had told them about our capture, and if they'd flown off to the States yet.

Everything in our lives had been snatched away from us in one swift moment. No one cared that Martin was an excellent pilot, or that I could make a great pizza. We were no longer defined by our ministry or careers; we were just two human beings in the middle of the Sulu Sea with no idea of what would happen next, and no way to influence it.

I sat there and watched the Abu Sayyaf talking to Martin, ordering him around, and thought to myself, *You guys don't even realize what a neat person he is. You've got this great guy sitting among you, and you don't even care.*

The boat's engine conked out from time to time, and guys went below deck to fiddle with it. Sometimes only after they let it cool off did it start again. One night during low tide, we ran aground on a sandbar. It took a lot of work to free us, and I worried about getting stuck there indefinitely. Another night it rained hard for a short time, so all twenty of us hostages retreated to the engine room.

One afternoon, the hostage group amused itself with more singing. "Somebody think of a Disney musical. . . . *Mary Poppins?* Okay, what are all the individual songs?" And then we'd sing "A Spoonful of Sugar," "Let's Go Fly a Kite," and anything else we could remember.

Chito, who came from a similar church environment as Martin and me, joined us in singing hymns: "Praise Ye the Lord, the Almighty," among others. The Abu Sayyaf tolerated our singing, for the moment anyway; they assumed it meant we were happy and content, whereas they hated to see us cry.

Sometime that day, dolphins began to follow the boat, jumping gracefully into the air. The blue of the water was exquisite, almost metallic. It was such a beautiful sight. We oohed and aahed with each leap. I couldn't help thinking that under different circumstances, this would be a wonderful cruise. The only problem was that Martin, without his glasses, couldn't see the marvelous show of nature at all.

At last on Wednesday evening, we found ourselves drawing close to land. The lights of a big city loomed on the horizon of one island. We hostages still had no idea where we were.

We began trolling up and down the coastline, looking for a flashlight signal from the shore that would indicate to the Abu Sayyaf a safe place to disembark. But the signal never came. So far as we could tell, we were truly alone.

7
HOSPITAL OF HORROR

(May 31–June 3, 2001)

THE ABU SAYYAF SEEMED convinced that they were in the right area, and so they maneuvered among some small islands to wait out the daylight hours of Thursday. Getting off the water after five days and four nights would indeed be a relief for us all. But what would we find once we stepped onto firm soil? Would conditions be better or worse?

During the afternoon, some Abu Sayyaf support people came out in a small boat. They found out what we needed, went back to shore, and then showed up again with cookies and Coke. Later that evening, we went back along the coast to search again for a flashlight signal. This time it came—two lights, in fact.

The shoreline at that place was rocky, and the fishing vessel couldn't get all the way in. So we all unloaded into water that was about chest-deep, like marines hitting the beaches of Normandy or something. Only we didn't feel nearly as brave.

More Abu Sayyaf were there on land to greet the comrades. Once again the cry of *"Allah akbar!"* went up, accompanied by the traditional double-kiss greeting, one to each cheek. *"Salam! Salam!* [Peace! Peace!]" echoed through the air. There was a lot of laughing and talking in languages I couldn't comprehend.

Then they started us up the hill in the dark. Not a house, not a campfire—nothing pierced the darkness at all. For some reason,

Martin had lost his *tsinelas* in the boat; he was now barefoot. It was just as well, because I found that the steep trail was too rough for my *tsinelas* anyway. They kept sliding around to the top of my feet, so I finally took them off. Most others did the same.

At the top, we came to a little shelter built for coconut husks, elevated about a foot off the ground. These structures are made so that a fire can be built underneath, in a pit, and the husks can be cooked into a form of charcoal. Meanwhile, the coconut meat inside the shelter is smoked, which preserves it for transporting to market.

This one was maybe twelve feet square. We climbed inside and lay down to sleep for the night on the split-bamboo floor. It had just a little give to it—a small improvement over the rigid deck of the ship. However, now that we were back on land, the mosquitoes were back with a vengeance.

We were all grimy, and when the morning light broke, we were thrilled to hear that we would be taken to the river, a few at a time, for baths. Letty, Kim, and Lalaine were the first to go, while the rest of us waited in the forest.

I need to stop here and clarify what the word *bath* means in this context. Put out of your mind all images of hot water, bubbles, or privacy. What I mean instead is stepping into a cold river fully clothed (so as not to be indecent before the watching guards), washing yourself under your clothing as best you can, coming out looking like a drowned rat, pulling a *malong* up around yourself to the point that you can hold one edge in your teeth, then fumbling around underneath trying to shed the wet clothes and put on dry ones—assuming that you have any. Otherwise, you just dry off gradually in the sun.

Letty and the girls had just started bathing when suddenly, without warning, gunfire erupted. The Armed Forces of the Philippines (AFP) had found us within just a few hours of landing onshore. I heard someone scream, "Drop!" and we all hit the jungle floor. I began to crawl on my stomach, using my forearms for traction, back toward the coconut shelter. The Abu Sayyaf immediately began to return fire, running into the forest to press the battle.

"Run, run, run!" came another command, and I stood up and began to run with my head down. I was petrified, my heart thumping through my chest. Several times we were interrupted with the order to drop; then we got up and ran again. Back in the shelter, we flopped down to catch our breath. Soon Letty and the girls stumbled in, absolutely panicked.

As the shots continued to ring out, Sabaya came into the shelter, looking specifically for Tess. "Come with us," he said. "We want you to call the radio station and give a message to President Arroyo. You tell her to call off the troops on Basilan and stop the indiscriminate shooting of the Abu Sayyaf, because they're going to injure innocent hostages."

Basilan—so that's where we were. For the first time in five days, Martin and I knew our location, although the name didn't ring a bell. Basilan, we learned later, is a small island only about forty miles across, just off the tip of Mindanao's Zamboanga Peninsula. Heavily wooded, it's a poor island to start with, made all the worse since the Abu Sayyaf sprang up in the early 1990s and established their stronghold here. Fear and chaos have since become the daily reality.

Tess did as instructed, using the sat-phone. Whether her message was immediately heard by decision makers or not, we don't know. But after some ten minutes, the shooting stopped. Amazingly, no one in our group was injured.

We sat in the coconut shelter trying to calm our nerves for a while. I had obviously never been shot at in my life, and neither had most of the other hostages. What a jolt to be going along in my day and suddenly find myself in mortal danger!

If someone had told me that this was the first of seventeen eventual firefights over the next months, I think I would have died on the spot.

As our nerves began to settle, one of the captors cooked a

big pot of rice and passed it down the line of hostages. Each of us reached in and grabbed a handful. I was still so tense I really didn't feel hungry, but I took some anyway. I knew I'd better seize the opportunity to gain nutrition while it was available. The pot was passed back and forth several times. The outside of the pot was blackened from having been placed over an open fire, so our hands were soon covered with black soot. There was no place to clean up, however; instead, we were quickly herded out the door and down the trail to another site, since the AFP knew we were here.

Less than an hour later, we stopped. Angie, Fe, and I really needed to use the bathroom. We weren't sure what to do, with so many men around us, so we just went off into some tall grass. Meanwhile, the Abu Sayyaf began rigging up their hammocks to some trees.

But then, for some reason or another, they decided this wasn't a good spot after all, and we were put back on the trail. As we hiked farther into the jungle, the terrain became much rougher and heavily forested. When we sat down for a rest again, we were attacked by a nasty swarm of bees. People jumped up and began to run and scream, even though the captors tried to get us to calm down. Several hostages got stung and began to cry.

The whole morale of the group plunged in that moment, as we realized that everywhere we turned, things were only getting worse. Fear wrapped itself around me. *How is this ever going to end?* I wondered. Darkness fell, and as we continued walking, they roped our wrists together like a chain gang. Martin was in front of me, Chito behind. We plodded on single file for another couple of hours and finally came to another coconut hut. This one, unlike the first, was full of husks; we had no choice but to sit on top of them, which was very uncomfortable.

A few civilians were around, and we could sense the tension in the air—something was going to happen. From the few pieces of English thrown into the conversations around us, we knew they were talking about a jeepney. Close to eleven o'clock, one rumbled up, and we were all herded onto it in the pitch-blackness—except for Sonny, Eldren, and Armando, the three Dos Palmas employees, for whom there simply wasn't space.

"Just keep them here," a guard directed.

The Abu Sayyaf piled onto the roof and we headed out. As we pulled away, one of the hostages said, "I wonder what's going to happen to Sonny. . . ." We learned much later that he and Armando were both beheaded within hours. Eldren was subjected to the same attempt, but it was botched. He escaped with his life, and a major neck scar.

The first driver was obviously inexperienced and went barreling down the bumpy trail at way too fast a speed, jostling all of us inside and perilously bouncing the guards above. One even fell off, as I recall. Sabaya soon took over the wheel, although he had trouble shifting the gears as well.

After an hour or so, we began to see houses and lights. We were coming to a town. Suddenly, we screeched to a stop under some lights. "Move, move, move!" came the order from a guard, who wanted us to get out of the jeepney as quickly as possible.

There was only one problem: We were still all tied together by the rope. The first person tried to step down, but the cord was all tangled, and our exit turned into a big pileup on the ground. The guards continued to scream at us, "Move! Move! Move!" obviously upset that we were wasting precious time. Eventually, we stumbled out onto the ground and were directed toward a small, one-story, U-shaped hospital. Later we learned the name of the town: Lamitan.

My heart sank. *This is the last thing this place needs!* I thought. *Patients are already sick and trying to get well—and here in the middle of the night comes a bunch of terrorists with their captives. Now even more lives are going to be endangered.*

Three of our captors—Hurayra, Bro, and Zacarias—began bashing out the jalousie windows with their gun butts. I think they were just trying to intimidate the staff with the noise of the shattering glass. They ushered us hostages from the courtyard into a one-bed patient room that happened to be unoccupied.

"Start taking baths," we were told, since this place finally afforded soap and freshwater—well, at least cold water. Someone suggested we should go alphabetically. Of course, we Burnhams loved that idea!

But by the time Martin and I got into the washing area, gunfire had erupted outside again. The hospital was getting blasted. This was a surprise to the Abu Sayyaf; they really didn't think the government troops would have the nerve to fire on a hospital. Their plan had been to stage this confrontation and thus force negotiations. I think they figured that after some talking and compromising, they would get concessions from Manila, the hostages would be released, and we would all go on our way.

But clearly, things weren't going according to plan. The AFP didn't care that this was a hospital and did not hold off as expected.

Martin and I dumped water over ourselves very quickly and got out. As for clothes, we had no choice but to put our dirty sets back on. We sat down in a corner to wait, choosing a spot on the floor far away from the door, just in case hostile forces came bursting in. As the gunfire ebbed and surged, one of the other hostages pointed to the windows just over our heads and told Martin and me we'd better move to a safer spot in the room. We did, now watching the door and windows closely. In the midst of this chaos, believe it or not, one of the captors poked his head in the room and handed us some Cokes and "biscuits" (cookies). We ate quickly, but with gratitude.

Imam, an elderly man with a goatee, stood guard at our door. His eyes crinkled when he smiled, and I thought he looked like somebody's nice grandpa. However, he was Abu Sayyaf nonetheless, and several of his family members belonged to the group as well.

I studied him as he stood by the door, gun in hand. *Why is he sitting here?* I wondered. *He's too old for heavy fighting. Maybe his job is just to wait and watch . . . and if things go badly tonight, he'll be the one to shoot us all?*

I nudged Martin and pointed to Imam. "Do you think he's been given the order to shoot us if things go wrong tonight?" I whispered.

True to his nature, my husband saw things differently. "Oh, no," he assured me. "I don't think anyone's planning to kill us. What they want from us is money."

• • •

As the wee hours of the night wore on, the fighting intensified, and we were moved into another room, this one with two patients lying in their beds. I'm embarrassed to admit what happened next. The other hostages promptly began to loot the room, taking everything from baby powder to soap to the patients' clothing. We had suddenly become as unscrupulous as our captors. The law of "I need this, so I'm taking it right now, whether it's mine or not" held sway.

What's the difference between us and the Abu Sayyaf? I said to myself. *We're all stealing.* Someone held out a toiletry item to me. "I'm not taking that," I answered. "It's not mine. We're stealing from these people!" The other hostages continued to get cleaned up in this patient room, while the rest of us sat outside on the floor along the hallway. As I sat there, I pondered what I had just witnessed. Up to this point, I had assumed we hostages were "the good guys." Now I had to admit that when you're thinking only of yourself and your own needs, you'll do just about anything.

What I would have hotly denied that night in Lamitan, of course, was the prospect that before the year was out, I would behave in much the same way.

In time, nurses moved the two patients out to other rooms in order to give us their space entirely. They also brought us some hospital scrubs to wear, which we gladly accepted. Martin finally got to change his shirt.

The gun battle continued throughout the rest of the night. The sun came up that Saturday morning, and we were exhausted from no sleep. Yet the firing continued. Some kind of aircraft arrived overhead and began to fire mortars at the hospital; one of them hit the operating room. A canister of oxygen exploded, starting a fire. Several of the Abu Sayyaf went running to fight the fire, while their comrades continued shooting.

Some time later, we were moved again back into the hallway, perhaps because it was more interior. Imam continued to sit and watch us, cradling his M16. Bro, a big, muscular warrior type with long and unusually wavy hair, came running back through the hall to rejoin the battle after fighting the fire. As he tiptoed between people's legs and bodies, he kept saying, "Excuse me . . . excuse me . . . excuse me." Martin and I looked at each other and couldn't help but chuckle at the display of politeness amid the carnage. It was so typical of Filipino courtesy.

By now the AFP had cut off the hospital's electricity and phone service. This infuriated the Abu Sayyaf, of course, who had hoped to use the phones to call the press and set up interviews.

Martin was summoned to the courtyard to make another communication on the sat-phone; signals were clearer out there. It made me nervous to have him leave my side, and especially to venture outside. But there was no choice.

"Call your mission in Manila," said Sabaya. "Tell them to call the American embassy, and have *them* call President Arroyo." The message was to be in the same vein as before: Stop firing on the hospital; you're endangering not only hostages but patients as well.

As Martin stood outside with the phone pressed to his ear, he soon heard the familiar voice of our friend Bob Meisel, NTM office chief in Manila. Bob didn't recognize Martin's voice at first, and it took a while to convince him that it was really Martin on the phone. Meanwhile, gunfire echoed in the background. There was no chance for honest talk, of course. Martin could only deliver his message as ordered.

"Martin, is Gracia with you?" Bob wanted to know.

"Yes, she is."

"Can I talk to her?"

"Well, she's not right here beside me. She's inside the hospital."

In the background, Sabaya kept saying to Martin, "Remind them that the Geneva Convention prohibits hostilities against hospitals!" Martin did as instructed. But it was all he could do to keep a straight face. It seemed so ironic—here was Sabaya, a radical terrorist, lecturing official governments on the rules of engagement as spelled out in the Geneva Convention!

By this point, the phone battery was dying, and the conversation ended abruptly.

Somehow in the middle of all this confusion, the Abu Sayyaf got word that Reggie and Rizza's ransom money had arrived. Since we were in such a public place, it would be easy to recruit a civilian to take them out of the hospital.

The captors decided that Divine's little boy, R. J., should be released as well. They had said on more than one occasion that R. J. was an "innocent" and should never have been kidnapped in the first place. When he learned that he was going to have to leave his mother, R. J. was terrified and began to cry. But Divine encouraged him, telling him it was for the best and that she would join him soon.

She struggled to stay calm—we all did—as we watched him leave the hospital with Reggie and Rizza. These events motivated the other hostages to get back on the sat-phone and try to make their own arrangements for release.

The day wore on, and the shooting raged without abatement. We ached for quiet so we could finally sleep, but that was not to be. My nervousness began to show itself in diarrhea, but a trip to the bathroom meant crossing the main corridor that opened to the front entrance—an open-fire zone. I took the chance a few times but then grew afraid to risk it.

"Is there another bathroom I can use?" I asked one of the nurses.

There was, inside an unoccupied patient room. As I entered the room, who should I see sleeping comfortably on the bed but an Abu Sayyaf member! Now I had a new worry: *What happens if he wakes up while I'm in the bathroom?*

I ducked back out to tell Martin. "I'm going to go ahead and use the bathroom in there," I told him. "But if I don't come back within a couple of minutes, you need to come looking for me, okay?" He promised he would.

Despite the gunfire all around, the nursing staff tried to manage the situation as best they could, even though I know they were scared themselves. They provided blankets for us to cover ourselves with when glass shards began to fly from the shooting. That was a good thing—except that under the blankets it was absolutely sweltering. It was about this time that someone named Sniper, a guide who knew Lamitan well and served the Abu Sayyaf, got shot directly in the eye. He was brought in from outside and laid in the hallway where we were all sitting. Blood poured from his face, and he moaned pitifully.

Nurses came over and began to bandage his eye. His breathing grew heavy and labored. Suddenly, his head turned to one side and he began to vomit blood onto the floor. As if in reply, the artillery from the sky grew all the louder. We watched in horror and sadness as Sniper writhed in agony.

A hospital staffer came into the hallway carrying T-shirts from the local school, which other hostages quickly grabbed. He also had a number of half-kilo bags of brown sugar. I didn't take one because I wasn't sure what I would do with brown sugar all by itself. (I hadn't yet learned to hoard any food I could grab at any time.)

The staffer dropped the sugar bags onto the floor. A couple of them burst open, and I watched as the brown granules mixed with the vomit. Suddenly the roar of the shelling ratcheted up, and someone cried, "Drop!" We all hit the deck. For the next thirty minutes, I lay on the floor, my face pointed directly into Sniper's sugar-soaked, bloody mess. It was almost more than I could bear.

Is this what it's like to watch someone die? I asked myself. I felt my mind starting to cloud over; I could no longer think straight. I was slipping into shock.

Glass began to fly through the air, and someone threw a blanket over me. I huddled there and knew I had to try to pull myself together. I gasped a prayer. *Oh, God, help me! Calm me down, please. Keep us safe, and keep me sane.*

The heat and the smells were unbearable. I got to the point I couldn't stand it anymore, and I threw off the blanket.

"What's wrong?" Martin asked.

"If I die, I die—but that blanket is going to suffocate me. It makes me feel claustrophobic under there," I told him.

• • •

By now it was late afternoon. Our emotions were drained. Even the Abu Sayyaf were pulling out their prayer beads to recite their pleas. I watched them as they silently prayed, their fingers working through the colored beads. Each rosary (the Muslims also called their beads a rosary) was made up of three sections of thirty-three beads each, plus one special addition on the end, making one hundred in all.

I couldn't help but feel as if this hospital was going to be our tomb. I looked at Martin and said, "They're just going to gun us all down. We're all going to die here."

Again, Martin reassured me. "I'm not so sure of that," he said. "It's got to end soon." Just then, out of nowhere, a new jeep pulled right up into the courtyard. Out jumped six or seven Abu Sayyaf reinforcements with guns and new ammunition! Immediately, the whole tone changed.

"How did you guys get through the roadblocks?" one of our captors asked incredulously.

"We just told them we were the governor's bodyguards." The governor of Basilan was, in fact, a former Abu Sayyaf who had hatched the kidnap-for-ransom strategy back in the beginning of the movement. He had since turned to politics, so he was no longer appreciated by his former comrades. But he still remembered how to organize his own personal army, his own jail, and so forth. At any rate, the mention of his name was enough to get this jeep through the AFP checkpoint.

Within half an hour came a new order: "Everybody start packing up! We're leaving!" I picked up a nearby sheet and formed a makeshift knapsack for Martin's extra shirt, our toothbrush, and a few pieces of leftover food. Some of the other hostages were eating a bit of rice, but I was too emotionally distraught to eat.

Before we left, the Abu Sayyaf began to divide up the group, picking out certain people to be released to work on ransom arrangements on behalf of their partners. For example, Janice was selected while Chito was told he'd be staying. Letty was chosen, but not her daughter and niece. Tess was picked, but not Francis. As they prepared to leave, Janice, Letty, and Tess were given instructions on how to send money to a contact point in Zamboanga City. They were told that if they did so, their loved ones would be freed.

After another emotional parting, the three left in one direction, while the remaining eleven of us were retied with rope in groups of three or so, then herded out the back, accompanied by Abu Sayyaf. I was amazed to see Sniper get to his feet and walk out with the rest of us.

Meanwhile, four new hostages were added to our group: three nurses named Ediborah, Reina, and Sheila, and an orderly named Joel.

In the courtyard, a breeze brushed across my face, and I found myself thinking, *Thank you, Lord—at least I'm going to die outside where it's a little cooler.*

I didn't have much time to reflect, however, as the shooting started up again. "Drop! Drop!" came the signal. Then "Run!" Then "Drop!" again.

We dropped near one house that had a little store attached to it. Bro bashed in the door with his foot and, with gunfire raging on all sides, coolly went inside to scoop up candy from the little jugs. He stuffed his pockets, then came back out and moved along the line of us on the ground, dropping a few pieces in front of each of us.

How weird is this! I thought to myself. *We're in the middle of a firefight, and he's thinking about candy.* We ran again and then were commanded to drop. I found myself lying between Martin and Guillermo. I looked up and saw the flash of a grenade over my shoulder, accompanied by a sudden burst of heat. Guillermo cried out, "I'm hit! I'm hit!"

Martin was very quiet. I turned to him and asked, "Did you get hit, too?"

"Yeah, in my back. But I can't tell if it's bad or not."

In the distance, I could hear Divine and Buddy calling out the same distress. "We've been hit!" they cried. "Just leave us, just leave us," Buddy told the captors. "We're wounded very badly."

One of the Abu Sayyaf said to another, "Just leave 'em."

It would have been nice if they had simply left us all behind at that moment. However, we were not so fortunate. One of the captors came over, looked at Martin's back, and quickly announced, "You're fine." Next he looked at Guillermo's wounded foot and again declared, "It's not serious. Let's go!"

We had no choice but to jump up and run again.

As we got to the edge of town, we slowed to a walking pace and began our second straight night of travel. Guillermo hobbled in pain. Martin's shrapnel wound proved not to be serious and eventually scabbed over. (Later on during our captivity, we heard on the news that Buddy and Divine had escaped from the jungle and had recovered from their wounds after a couple of months in the hospital.) Every hour or hour and a half, we stopped for a rest. Each time I was so exhausted I just sank down on the ground and instantly fell asleep. They woke us when it was time to march on again.

Oddly, the AFP didn't pursue us. As time went on, we noticed that they never pursued us. A battle was one thing, but pressing on for capture didn't seem to be on their agenda. This was one of the continuing mysteries of our ordeal.

We got to a hill beside a farmhouse, and as we looked far across the valley, we could see a firefight underway. Tracers were exploding in the sky.

"What is that?" we asked Sabaya.

"It's a gun battle our guys started over there to draw the AFP away from us," he explained.

We lay down under a tree, the first of many nights we slept on the cold ground. By this time, Angie was hysterical without her sister Divine. She was in such bad shape that I said to Martin, "Maybe I ought to sleep beside her tonight, just to help her through." He nodded.

I brought the sheet I had picked up at the hospital and spread it out for Angie and me. I found two stones to serve as pillows, almost like Jacob of the Old Testament had done. "Everything's going to be okay," I murmured to her as I tried to comfort her. "I'll stay with you tonight. I know you'll miss Divine and Buddy, but it's better that they aren't with us. They're free, Angie. . . ." I kept my arm around her through the rest of the night.

The next morning, however, Martin admitted that he had just about frozen during the night alone. He needed me, and I wasn't there for him. I cried and cried as I thought about my husband lying all alone, shivering in the cold. *From this moment on, I vowed, I will never leave his side when it is time to sleep, no matter what the circumstances.* I kept that pledge all the way to the end.

8
THE THREAT

(June 3–7, 2001)

The Abu Sayyaf leaders had spent the night inside the farmhouse, while the other captors had strung their hammocks between the piers that supported it, up off the ground. That morning they killed a goat and boiled it to go along with our usual rice for breakfast.

While we were grateful for the nutrition, the meat proved to be extremely tough. We chewed and chewed and chewed, then finally just swallowed it whole.

Outside the farmhouse, Sabaya found a pair of old, holey boots made of bright blue vinyl—what some people call gum boots or rain boots. They had slits in the back, and the soles were starting to separate from the top. "Do you want these?" he asked me, holding them up.

They looked as if they were falling apart, so I declined them in favor of my *tsinelas.* He moved on to offer the boots to others, but nobody else wanted them either.

Soon he came back around to me. "Sure you don't want these?" he asked.

I thought I might be able to find a use for them later, so I told Sabaya I'd take them.

By this time, somebody in the group had given Martin a pair of Boston polo slippers, a type of fairly substantial rubber sandal. We left the farmhouse and began walking again that day. While we were fording a brook, the current swept away one of my *tsinelas* and I promptly switched to the new boots. I breathed a silent prayer of thanks to God for giving me a second chance at taking them. I actually ended up wearing them for the next eleven months. I may have looked like a milkmaid just coming out of the barn, but at least I wasn't barefoot.

About a week later, my guard lost one of his *tsinelas* in the water as well. I gave him my extra one so he'd have a "matching" set.

As we hiked through the jungle trails, we saw *alimatok* (leeches) everywhere. These thin little inch-long things look like worms and sit on leaves waving around, looking for something to grab. When they fasten onto your skin, they begin to suck blood, swelling up in the process.

At every rest along the trail, I'd pull off my boots to inspect for *alimatok*. I got to the point that whenever I felt a slight itch on some part of my foot or leg, I knew right away it was probably an *alimatok*.

There's a certain kind of *alimatok* that goes straight for your eyes. If not quickly removed, it can cause blindness. We learned to be especially vigilant against these.

• • •

Meanwhile, guns and weapons were everywhere. More than once I found myself with a captor sitting across from me, his M16 casually pointed straight in my direction. I would gently reach out and nudge the barrel to one side or the other.

One fellow saw that this was bothering me, so he was nice enough to reach down and place his finger over the end of the barrel! *That's really good!* I thought to myself. *First his finger will get shot off—and THEN I'll die!* Finally I just gave up and accepted that having guns pointed at me was going to be a never-ending hazard.

Early June
U.S. State Department and FBI advise politicians inquiring into the kidnapping to say little in public, so as not to raise the Burnhams' "market value" in the Abu Sayyaf's eyes.

At night, we began to see a spy plane patrolling the sky above us, apparently looking for campfires. We didn't know whether it was Philippine or a loaner from the U.S. military. Martin thought it sounded like an unmanned craft, and his knowledge of airplanes was considerable. Back and forth the plane searched. Every time we heard the plane approaching, we'd stop walking and stand perfectly still, so as not to draw attention. Once the plane passed, we'd continue on.

The Abu Sayyaf didn't want to be recognized by the armed forces, of course. And neither did we. Why? Because we knew by now that a frontal attack to rescue us would probably turn out badly. The AFP wanted to help us hostages, but pulling off an operation that sensitive was simply beyond their training. At this point, we knew that our only real hope of getting out alive lay instead in negotiation. And for the Abu Sayyaf, negotiation meant only one thing: ransom money.

We saw few if any civilians along the way; they mainly fled whenever fighting broke out. As a result, we passed through one deserted village after another. It was eerily quiet.

At a certain time every night, a commercial airliner would pass overhead, its wing lights blinking in the starry sky. Where it was headed, we could only wonder. Australia, perhaps? Lying there on the ground, we would gaze up, and I would say wistfully to Martin, "I wish I was on that plane. . . ."

"I wish I was, too," he'd quietly reply.

•   •   •

As the days passed, I was gradually learning the many uses of the *malong*. This piece of batik material is some forty inches wide and probably twice as long, with the two ends sewn together to form a large tube. You can step into it and roll it up around your waist to form a long skirt. You can pull it over yourself on cold nights for a blanket. You can use it as a towel or even a tissue when necessary. Whenever it's time to move, you can spread it out to become a knapsack for any belongings you're carrying. If someone is injured, you can turn it into a stretcher if you cut down a couple of tree saplings for poles.

When I stepped inside and pulled it up high to the point where I could grab the top edge with my teeth, I had a privacy curtain for changing clothes, with both my hands free. When it came to bathroom activity, I could also squat inside my *malong*. However, I wound up soiling mine more than a few times as I was learning. That meant trips to the river to wash it out.

One of the most difficult adjustments in the jungle was forcing myself to get along without toilet paper. The others seemed not to mind, but I really struggled. To clean up after a bowel movement with only cold water and my hand was almost more than I could take. And occasionally, there wasn't even any water to use.

The next mealtime, when I had to eat with only my hands, I almost gagged.

Whenever we went through a stream, the guys refilled the water jugs. For some reason, I found that I especially needed a lot of water when we were "mobiling," the Abu Sayyaf term for hiking. Otherwise, my face would get really red and my breathing would intensify, scaring the others.

I found that if I asked for a drink at certain times of the day, the Abu Sayyaf got very irritated with me. Sometimes they said a flat no. It took me a while to figure out that they were saving the water for the ritual washing that preceded their three prayer times each day— dawn, 12:30 p.m., and sundown.

Those on jihad are excused from two of the five daily prayer times normally required of Muslims. However, an additional prayer time is expected of them at 1 or 2 a.m. Our guys never did it; they

---

June 4
About half a dozen men begin meeting at Rose Hill Bible Church from 6:00 to 6:30 a.m. to pray for the Burnhams' release. They continue six days a week for more than a year.

were too tired after long days of mobiling. Once when the group was feeling a lot of pressure from the military, there was a discussion about whether the lack of this prayer was the reason. They tried to get up in the middle of the night a few times to pray but soon lapsed.

Before they could recite their prayers, the captors went through the washing ritual. Every day, three times a day, they did this. The ritual consisted of:

1. Washing their right hand and arm up to their elbow—*twice*
2. Washing their left hand and arm up to their elbow—*twice*
3. Washing their face—*twice*
4. Washing their ears
5. Washing their mouth by taking in a sip of water and then spitting it out
6. Sniffing water up their nose and then blowing it out
7. Patting water onto their hair
8. Washing their feet

(I must confess that the constant spitting and blowing of mucus was not exactly my favorite thing.)

All of this activity consumed a fair amount of water, naturally, and the captors took it very seriously. One evening, we were getting ready to eat and Angie accidentally brushed up against one of the guys after he had washed for prayer. "Why did you touch me?!" he erupted. "Now I'm unclean, and I have to go start my washing all over again!" This meant waiting in a long line at the mountain spring we were using in that place in order to refill his jug. He was thoroughly frustrated as he stomped away.

• • •

A couple of days after we escaped from the hospital in Lamitan we came to another abandoned house. Several of the Abu Sayyaf, along with some of the male hostages, moved into the living room, giving us women a smaller room off to the side.

Just as we were settling in, I heard someone yelling, "*Sundalo! Sundalo!* [Soldiers! Soldiers!]" The army was coming once again. We hadn't spent even one night in this place. We scurried to collect our stuff for another dash into the woods.

But as we gathered to get ready to go, I noticed that Martin's shoes were missing. I got upset. Who would have stolen them?

"Don't worry about it," he said. "I'm sure they'll turn up."

"What do you mean?" I retorted. "We're going to have to go into the forest again, and you don't have anything to wear on your feet."

I approached Musab, who seemed to be the leader of our particular cluster. "Martin needs his shoes," I announced, with little attempt to restrain my anger.

Always slightly aloof, Musab looked around casually and then just shrugged.

Now I was really ticked off. "Martin can't walk through the forest in bare feet!" I lectured. "You've got to get him some shoes. This is ridiculous. He's going to get injured, and you have to do something about it. Do you understand me?"

All of a sudden, it dawned on me: No, he *didn't* understand me, because he knew very little English.

His face grew stern at being reprimanded by a mere woman. He turned and walked away. (I later found out Musab was the second in command of all the Abu Sayyaf!)

Solaiman came over and said, "Gracia, you need to calm down. This will all work out."

At just that moment, Musab's brother came walking up the hill from where we had been taking baths—and he was wearing Martin's Boston polos! I was fit to be tied. The guy had even broken them in one place. With a big smile on his face, he calmly handed them back to Martin without a word of explanation.

I was really angry, but gradually I settled down. I realized that if I wanted to get out alive and see my kids again, I'd better get a grip on my temper.

We walked all afternoon and toward evening stopped at another coconut hut to sleep. But just before sundown, *sundalo* were spotted again. So we took refuge on top of a ridge. When gunfire erupted at the bottom of the hill, several Abu Sayyaf ran down to engage the enemy.

They returned later, exulting in their achievement. We learned that they had beheaded three AFP soldiers and ransacked their belongings. One of the victims had been a medic. They brought back his medical bag for our future use.

Another had the company radio. Along with the radio, they found detailed paperwork that outlined the AFP's full strategic plan for seeking the Abu Sayyaf, complete with detailed maps. The goals were enumerated and included a list of all the battalions deployed in this effort.

Chito stared at the list and exclaimed, "Look at all the people looking for us!" We'd had no idea the deployment was this large. Obviously, we were in the crosshairs of a major military operation. Unfortunately, that thought was not comforting at all.

In this particular skirmish, several Abu Sayyaf members had been wounded and one was killed. His comrades cut down small trees to make poles, and by using *malong*s, they put together stretchers for the casualties. When we passed through a Muslim village during the night, they left both the dead and the wounded. The rest of us walked onward all night long once again.

The next morning, we stopped to rest. The nurses who had joined us at Lamitan tended to those with smaller injuries.

We continued this trek for several days. Along the way, Martin and I finally learned who the real Abu Sayyaf leader was. He had been part of our group from the time we landed on Basilan, but we didn't suspect, from his quiet way and his baby face, that Khadafi Janjalani was the man in charge. He also used the name Moktar.

Janjalani's older brother, Abdurajik Abubakar Janjalani, had founded the group more than a decade earlier, after returning from the Afghan jihad that evicted the Soviets back in 1989. Inspired by his Islamic professor there, whose name was Abdul Rasul (Abu) Sayyaf, the older Janjalani had settled in his hometown on Basilan to start up a similar effort. The AFP had finally gunned him down in December 1998, and now his younger brother had inherited the mantle.

Our group kept getting bigger and bigger. One day around noon, we came upon a school. Although classes weren't in session, there were a few teachers around, and for some reason they weren't afraid of us. We all looked a mess by this time, and we could tell they felt sorry for us. They graciously had someone in the community kill a cow, which they prepared for us. Boiled eggs, Maggi brand noodles, rice, and hot sweet milk were all added to the menu—a feast! It was the first real meal we had enjoyed in a week, since leaving the boat.

The ladies also gave me a change of clothes: some pants, a long-sleeved shirt, a bra, more underwear—and even an expensive green Penshoppe hand towel! The other women hostages received similar outlays. We were overwhelmed with their kindness. I tucked everything into my sheet knapsack, which I always carried either in my hand or over my shoulder.

We stayed long enough at the school to eat and catch a few minutes' rest before heading back into the jungle. Not long after that, we arrived at a place I dubbed "House 125," which is what the leftover census sticker on the front wall of the house said. A two-room hovel with a thatched roof, it had no electricity, no plumbing, and no glass or even screen in the window openings. It was elevated on stilts some five feet off the ground, like most rural houses in the tropics, and it was accessible by a wooden ladder. The space underneath the house was designed as a place to keep pigs and

---

June 5
Martin's brother Brian, his wife, Arlita, and their family arrive in Rose Hill from their mission post in Papua New Guinea to give support during the crisis.

---

chickens—although now, with no animals around, some of the terrorists used it for their hammocks, slinging them from the supporting poles. Others tied up to nearby trees.

To the Abu Sayyaf, this was a safe haven: remote enough to avoid the armed forces that prowled in search of them, yet close to villages and farms with food supplies and a river only a few minutes' walk away. Here they could use their sat-phones to keep up the media pressure on the Manila government to accede to their demands.

As we settled into the house, we hostages had a big discussion about how we would sleep. Our Muslim captors had made it clear that Martin and I, as a married couple, should be in the middle to serve as a dividing line between the sexes—something about preserving decency. Next to Martin came Guillermo, since our captors were handcuffing the two of them together each night so as not to lose their prime bargaining chips. The rest of that side included Francis, Chito, and Joel, the young hospital orderly.

Meanwhile, on my side came the three nurses: Sheila, Reina, and Ediborah. Beyond them were Angie and Fe. The teenagers, Kim and Lalaine, huddled up against the wall. We were crunched together so tightly that every time I'd wake up and want to turn over, I couldn't get leverage. It reminded me of being nine months pregnant and trying vainly to get comfortable during the night.

"Hey, I have an idea," I said after the first miserable night. "What if some of you sleep over here at the foot of the row in the extra space? We're not using that. How about you, Lalaine and Kim? This would be a good spot for you two."

They looked at me as if I were crazy. "We *can't* sleep there! Don't you know it's bad luck to sleep facing a door?" Almost every Filipino apparently knows that you have to sleep at a right angle to a doorway, or something terrible might happen to you.

"Okay, then Martin and I will do it. That will give everybody more space."

"No, no, no!" they all protested in unison. "You've been assigned to sleep in the line with all the rest of us." I could see I wasn't going to win this debate.

I woke up one morning and I could hear the birds twittering in the jungle trees and the *thwack* of wood being chopped for the cooking fires. The clanking of pots made me think there might be coffee this morning. At the same time, the mournful prayers of our captors droned on. They began the day with at least twenty minutes of this ritual.

I tried to smooth out my pair of brown *pantos,* which are like pajama bottoms, that someone had given me. I arranged my *terong,* or head shawl, so as to ward off the disapproving stares of our captors. I still didn't have a pair of socks.

Necessity being the mother of invention, however, I had come up with a substitute to protect my feet. A day or two before, Lalaine had said to me along the trail, "Would you like an extra shirt I found?"

"Oh, thank you!" I was thrilled at her thoughtfulness.

She tossed a garment my way—and it turned out to be a little girl's Brownie uniform, about the right size for an eight-year-old. I was disappointed. But after looking at it, I realized that if I tore off the two sleeves, I could pull them onto my feet, folding an end over each set of toes, and then I'd have some padding inside the old blue rubber boots.

Soon it was time for breakfast. A couple of the "boys"—young cadres still in their teens—brought in our food on a big banana leaf. The rice was piled high, with a can of sardines in tomato sauce dumped on top. There were no bowls or utensils for eating; we simply dug in with our hands—and quickly, I soon learned. We hostages were friends and allies of each other, except when it came to nutrition. If we didn't grab quickly, we went hungry.

June 6
An FBI team spends six hours in Rose Hill gathering information about the Burnhams for their case against the Abu Sayyaf.

Something about the frenzy just saddened me this particular morning. I couldn't force myself to get in there and fight for my food yet again. It made me feel like an animal. I sat over at the side of the room and watched the scramble, until Guillermo noticed.

"Come on, Gracia—time to eat! You've got to keep your strength up."

"I just don't want to grab," I replied.

Francis overheard me, and after the banana leaf was wiped clean, he came over to sit beside me, a pensive look on his face. "You know, my dogs at home eat better than this," he volunteered in a low voice.

"Well," I replied, "to be quite honest, this is exactly what we *do* feed our dogs—rice with a bit of sardines and tomato sauce."

Neither of us was really complaining. We were just reflecting on what was becoming of us here in the jungle, pawns in the dark drama of a desperate face-off. We knew the government in Manila viewed the Abu Sayyaf as nothing more than greedy thugs to be squashed. The fact that they held innocent bystanders as hostages was a complicating factor, to be sure. But the battle must go on.

The only trouble was, the Abu Sayyaf knew every valley and ridge of this rain-forested island far better than the AFP, and they were not about to be caught in the open.

The morning heat grew as the hours slowly passed. We were not allowed to leave the room; this had become our quarters twenty-four hours a day, unless we needed to go outside "for the call of nature," as Solaiman enjoyed phrasing it. He had learned the euphemism from an American acquaintance somewhere. He could be gracious toward us when he wanted to, although he harbored a smoldering resentment of the West—the fountain of all vice,

---

June 6
Jeff, Mindy, and Zach arrive in Rose Hill, escorted by their aunt and uncle, Cheryl and Walt Spicer. Everyone moves in with Paul and Oreta Burnham.

self-indulgence, immorality, and coarseness, in his view. He did appreciate his Levi's, however.

Chatter drifted up through the floor from the leaders' council that was meeting underneath the house. There was something about negotiations, which sounded hopeful. As I listened more closely, I realized that Sabaya—the flamboyant spokesman for the group to the outside world—was talking with someone on the sat-phone. But it was clear the discussion was not going well.

"No, we don't want Castillo to negotiate with us!" Sabaya snapped. "Who is he, anyway? We don't know him, and we don't trust him. We want Malaysia to come in and mediate this problem. That worked fine last time, with the people from Sipadan. You need to appoint someone from there."

(William Castillo, we learned later, was an appointee of President Arroyo; he had already offended Sabaya by being abrasive the first time they talked. So things started off on the wrong foot.)

I listened quietly, thinking to myself, *If President Arroyo is smart, she'll get a new negotiator. The personal chemistry has to be good if there's going to be any hope of compromise.* Another hour or so passed. I wondered, as I had done every day multiple times, what was happening with our three children. Had the mission flown them out of the country and back to the States yet? Who had told them in the beginning that Dad and Mom had been captured? Did they handle it sensitively? Were Jeff and Mindy and Zach falling apart by now? Jeff, fourteen, would try to be the strong older brother. But Mindy was only eleven, and Zach just ten. This was so awful. . . .

My thoughts were interrupted by the sound of Sabaya on the sat-phone again—this time with the president herself. "Madam President, it does not seem that you are getting the picture. We have three Americans. We need a million dollars for Martin. If we get that, we'll let him go free, and his companion, too."

Whatever she said in reply unleashed a forceful rebuttal. Before

long, Sabaya was almost shouting. "You want our unconditional sur-
render—what are you, crazy? If your generals think they can follow us
into the mountains and finish us off, they are out of their minds!"

Then in the heat of it all, Sabaya stormed, "If you don't let
Malaysia in here to mediate within seventy-two hours, we're going
to kill one of the whites!"

Martin and I looked at each other in shock. Was this a death
sentence for one of us? Was he really serious? The only "whites"—
according to Sabaya's definition—were the two of us and Guillermo.
(He had, in fact, been naturalized as a full American citizen only
twelve days before his capture. But as far as the Abu Sayyaf was
concerned, he was Yankee all the way.)

I looked over at Francis, who by now was sitting in a corner.
I raised my eyebrows as if to ask, *Did I hear correctly?* He looked
back at me but didn't nod.

When the phone call ended, I moved over beside Francis.

"Did I hear them say they're going to kill one of the whites?"
I whispered.

Francis nodded slowly and confirmed, "Yes, that's what you
heard," turning then to stare at the floor. There wasn't anything
left to say. We both knew that when the Abu Sayyaf used the word
"kill," they weren't just talking about a bullet to the chest. They
were talking about their trademark procedure, of which they were
very proud: beheading with a *bolo* knife, the Philippine equivalent
of a machete.

I rehearsed what I might say if they came and started to take
Martin away. I would tell them, "Take me, not Martin. My kids need
a father. I'm a mere woman—the family can do without me." I knew
that my captors didn't value me as highly as they did Martin, so
I thought I might be able to convince them to take me in his place.
On the other hand, the pragmatic side of my brain jumped in to
say, *Calm down, Gracia. Surely Sabaya is bluffing. Think about it:
His whole strategy depends on keeping you alive. You're too valuable
to sacrifice.*

Martin seemed to agree with this thought. "They need us to bargain with," he said quietly. "If they kill us, what will they have left?"

It was this idea that led us not to say anything to Guillermo, who hadn't heard the conversation below and therefore had missed the threat. We figured there was no need to raise undue alarm. But Martin and I both looked down at our watches to calculate the time when the seventy-two hours would expire: 3:15 on Sunday afternoon. That evening we quietly prayed together that God would somehow keep us safe and set us free.

9

LEFT BEHIND

(Rest of June 2001)

FRIDAY AND SATURDAY came and went without incident. We did very little other than sit in that hot little hut, talking and sharing stories. To relieve the boredom, Chito came up with brainteasers for us. One was about a river with three missionaries on one side and three headhunters on the other. A small boat was available, but it would carry only two people at a time. The goal was to get all of the missionaries across the river without their ever being outnumbered and thus put at risk.

We worked at the puzzle for hours, using little stones and a piece of wood as markers. I think we eventually even came up with a solution, although I can't remember what it is now. We told stories about ourselves, our families, our jobs. We summarized books we had read. When it was my turn, I told parts of the life of Christ. Then Martin went on and related the story of a missionary like us whose name was Paul. He talked about the places Paul went, the people he met, and the things he accomplished. We told "hostage stories" from the Bible, such as the account of the little servant girl from Israel who introduced the Syrian general Naaman to the one true God. We told the Queen Esther story—another person who didn't choose to be in the situation in which she found herself.

Others talked about what they hoped to do if they ever got released. Joel wanted to be a fireman, maybe even in the United

States. Fe wanted to go to college and learn about computers. Angie and I talked about the entertainment sites of Branson, Missouri. I told her Martin and I had honeymooned there and promised that when she came to visit me in the States, we'd take a trip to Silver Dollar City! We tried to comprehend the motivations of the Abu Sayyaf, and various opinions flowed back and forth.

At other times, my mind was pretty much consumed with the immediate trial of daily living. I struggled just to keep myself together. *Okay, I have to go to the bathroom, but I don't want to go out there in front of eighty men. Maybe I can wait a while longer. . . .*

Martin spent a lot of time with Guillermo those two days. He had already let us know he wasn't religious—"I really don't 'practice' " was his way of putting it. He was more preoccupied with wrapping up his divorce back home so he could marry Fe. But under the conditions, he had grown close to Martin and respected him as a friend.

"You know, Guillermo, we need to be ready for whatever comes," Martin said to him. He explained that all of us have done things that are wrong and that God, who is holy, considers these things to be sin. He told Guillermo that we can't save ourselves and that without God's mercy, we all face eternal death. This was one of several conversations Martin had had with him about the need for Christ's forgiveness and freedom from the captivity of sin.

Guillermo listened quietly. When darkness came, after the two of them had been handcuffed together once again, Guillermo said to Martin, "Thank you for all the things you've been telling me. You've really helped me a lot."

Sunday finally arrived. Sabaya's deadline passed without incident, amid a flurry of sat-phone conversations. Apparently, the government had agreed to some of the Abu Sayyaf's negotiation details. We didn't know the specifics, but we all breathed a little easier.

The next morning, which was Monday, some of the "boys" returned with a delivery of food. I looked down from our room toward the ground outside and was excited to see a pumpkin! We hadn't had vegetables for so long. There was also a goat or two tied up that would be cooked. My mouth began to water and I could almost taste the deliciousness to come.

Cooking fires were lit, and the preparation began. Just as they were getting ready to begin cooking the meat, gunfire erupted, as it had the previous weekend. This house wasn't a safe place after all. For the fourth time in less than two weeks, we'd been found by the AFP.

The Abu Sayyaf immediately began blasting back with their M16s, spraying bullets in every direction. Meanwhile, we hostages scrambled down the rickety ladder, clutching hastily gathered belongings in our hands. We huddled together under the house, wondering if these would be our final minutes on earth.

"Run!" came the order. We dashed up the hill, trying to get away from the advancing troops. I gasped for breath but could not stop; I had to keep going as fast as I could. As I ran through the jungle, I heard an unfamiliar sound. First there was a *thump!* Then a few seconds later, we heard a *shwoo woo woo* overhead. A short while later, I heard the same *thump!* But this time, the sound was followed by an explosion very close to where we were running. As we ducked down to avoid the blast, I realized what we were hearing: incoming artillery. Martin and I looked at each other in disbelief. "What in the world?" he exclaimed. "They're shooting artillery at us! They have to know the hostages are here—what's all this heavy firepower about?"

If this was the AFP's method for rescuing hostages, we were in deeper trouble than we had thought. The Abu Sayyaf had always wanted us to stay out of sight whenever soldiers were near, and now we quickly came to agree with them.

Martin turned to me and said, somewhat sarcastically, "These

June 10
An all-family prayer meeting is held at Paul and Oreta Burnham's home.

---

must be the most accurate artillerymen in the world; they think they can fire from ten miles away and kill Abu Sayyaf but avoid us?"

Once we got far enough away from the gunfire, we were finally able to slow to a walk. But we still needed to keep moving since we had no idea if the AFP was following us or not. Our hike that day was neither short nor easy; we had to make our own trails through the thick underbrush, uphill and downhill, until we were exhausted. We didn't stop until evening. It was dark when we finally got to a high place that the captors felt was safe. There we settled down for the night.

The Abu Sayyaf were clearly upset. Their threat hadn't worked. They'd hoped to get an acceptable negotiator on the scene—and instead, they were on the receiving end of bullets. The leaders huddled in agitated discussion.

Now what would they do? we wondered. As we looked around for a level place on the ground to sleep, a captor named Haija moved Martin over to a small tree. He didn't speak much English, but he made it clear that Martin should sit down on the ground and extend his arms around the tree, so that he could then snap on the handcuffs. "You'll sleep here," he announced. With his arms wrapped around the tree, Martin obviously couldn't lie down.

Once again, I spoke before I could stop myself. I turned to Mang Ben and said, "It's going to be very hard for him to sleep this way."

Mang Ben looked me straight in the eye. "*I—don't—care,*" he spat. I bit my tongue as I turned to my husband and said, "I promise I'll be right here, Martin. I'm not going to leave you."

Guillermo, who had been cuffed to Martin every night up to this point, was given a new restraint as well. They tied his hands behind his back with a rope and then said, "You come with us. Someone wants to see you."

Guillermo had removed his shirt earlier that evening in order to cool off. Now, as he was being led away, he tossed the pink pullover to me. Kicking his backpack in my direction, he said, "Take care of my stuff till I get back, okay?"

Oh, my goodness, I thought as I picked up the backpack. *This definitely does not sound good. Are they going to . . . ?* I didn't want to finish the sentence.

I feverishly racked my brain for a less frightening explanation. *Maybe his ransom has come through, and they just want to talk to him about a release,* I thought to myself, trying to put the best face on what was occurring.

About five minutes later, we heard scuffling and shouts from down the hill.

"I wonder what that was," I said to Martin, straining to hear more.

"Hmmm, I'm not sure."

"Maybe a civilian found our camp or something," I ventured. It was a lame guess, to be sure, and we both fell into an uneasy silence. Martin figured out a way to recline, while I huddled up against him in the cold. We prayed together, and as always, our thoughts turned to our kids. We tried to think what they might be doing at that moment. Monday night in the Philippines would be Monday morning in the United States; they were probably sleeping in, since it was summertime.

As our conversation slowed, I began to doze off and on but kept jerking awake, looking for Guillermo to come walking back into camp to claim his stuff. I finally used his backpack as a makeshift pillow, and in time, Martin and I both fell asleep.

The next morning, Guillermo was nowhere to be seen. We didn't want to ask, but his fiancée, Fe, couldn't hide her concern. "Where is Guillermo?" she demanded of the captors.

"He went with a striking force during the night," one of the men told her. As we looked around, that made some sense; there were perhaps twenty Abu Sayyaf missing from the group as well, and it was not uncommon for these groups to raid villages and raise havoc during the night. Maybe they had forced Guillermo to join them.

Later that day, however, I was watching a group of the remaining captors as they horsed around with each other, just having fun.

Somebody pushed a pleasant young man named Jaafar, who was probably no more than eighteen years old. In a slightly mocking tone, he retorted, "Oooh, oooh, don't kill me! I want to see my sons!"

What? It didn't make sense, at least in the present setting. But my intuition told me the sickening truth: *That was a quote right out of Guillermo's mouth.* I couldn't prove it, but somehow I knew I was right. I told Martin what I had just heard, and even though we hoped it wasn't so, we couldn't get the thought out of our minds that those may have been Guillermo's last words.

In the days to come, we heard that line repeated more than once; in fact, it became kind of an "in" joke among the captors. We gradually admitted to ourselves the awful truth: Guillermo's decapitated body was lying back there somewhere on a hillside, marked only by his head raised up on a bamboo pole like a trophy.

Sabaya had kept his word. The world had been shown that, indeed, this group was tough.

· · ·

A day or so after the murder, word arrived that Tess's work had been successful, and the money to release her husband, Francis, had come through. Young Kim's ransom had arrived as well.

This was not, in itself, a source of immediate joy, because the hazardous process of transfer was yet to be arranged. The Abu Sayyaf wanted to make sure the hostages did not fall into AFP hands. They kept working to find civilians they felt they could trust to spirit them across the seventeen-mile strait of water to Zamboanga, where they could make public statements.

June 17, Father's Day
Following a family tradition, the three kids pose for photos that they hope will reach their dad. Paul Burnham intentionally positions them with the Rose Hill house showing in the background, so Martin and Gracia will know where they are.

Meanwhile, we hostages who remained wrote up a list of supplies for Francis to send back to us if he could: some more *malong*s, deodorant, toothpaste, chocolates, etc.

"Tell the people out there they really need to work to get us out of here," we added.

"Oh, yes, we'll get you out," he replied. "Filipino businessmen will give money; we can come up with the ransom for you, too."

Several days before, I had found an optician's discount card in the bag of abandoned IDs we had retrieved back on the boat and had penned a quick note to our children on the back of it. I had kept it upbeat, not wanting to upset them any more than they probably already were.

> *Hey Kids,*
>
> *Wanted to say hello and let you know that we are fine. The Lord has given us special strength to hang in here when the going gets tough! We'll tell you all about it one day. Until then, we love you 3 w/ all our hearts. We have the best family!!*
>
> *Love, Mom & Dad*

Francis took this note, too, and it made it to our kids. Jeff had it laminated and still carries it in his wallet.

We hiked several hours until we reached another farmhouse. Here, Francis and Kim were turned over to couriers, again with detailed instructions of what to say. Francis was to stop at Radyo Agong and repeat the familiar grievances: "We want our homeland back. We will keep causing trouble for the government until they agree to negotiate. More and more hostages will be taken."

Francis did as instructed; his words were heard on the radio the very next day.

June 18
President Arroyo comes to Zamboanga City, meets with the hostages' relatives at a military base, and vows that no ransom will be paid.

Meanwhile, the Abu Sayyaf decided to split us into two groups. Ediborah, Sheila, Angie, and Fe were in one group. Our group included Chito, Joel, Reina, young Lalaine, Martin, and me. No reason was given for this split; perhaps it was just to complicate the AFP's task and not risk losing us all at once.

We didn't see each other for perhaps three weeks. During that time, we stayed by a really nice river, almost like a park. We rested and got a bath almost every day. We rigged up a *tolda,* a piece of multistriped plastic awning thrown over a rope between two trees and tied off at the corners to nearby bushes for shade.

Some logging was going on in that area, and we managed to scavenge some boards to lay down on the ground under our *tolda,* making a small platform for the five of us to sleep on and keep us out of the mud when it rained. (Joel had talked one of the Abu Sayyaf into giving him a hammock, which he strung nearby.)

A couple of the captors decided to hang their hammocks on the trees supporting our *tolda,* which perched them directly overhead, so low that we couldn't even sit up during the night. Talk about togetherness! But to the average Filipino, this wasn't unusual at all.

One day, Sabaya called each of us to meet with him for a reading from the Koran. Martin and I went together.

"I want to explain to you the meaning of my name, 'booty of war,'" he began. "You guys are our booty. We can make you slaves— but for now you're just our war booty. The Koran says we are allowed to do this. Here, you can read it for yourself." He handed an English translation to Martin.

My husband read the following passage: "So when you meet in battle those who disbelieve . . . when you have overcome them,

---

June 22
Gracia's sister-in-law, Beth Jones, and her boys come from Kansas City to visit the kids in Rose Hill. They go to the zoo and then the park; pictures taken on this day make it to their parents in the jungle.

---

then make prisoners, and afterwards either set them free as a favor or let them ransom [themselves]."

Other passages Sabaya showed us said, "Those who repent before you, have them in your power" and "Say to the infidels: If they desist, what is now past shall be forgiven them; but if they return, they have already before them the doom of the ancients. Fight then against them till strife be at an end, and the religion be all of it Allah's."

Sabaya then explained his interpretation, as outlined by various Muslim scholars: "There are four options that can be pursued with people who are the booty of war: (1) kill them; (2) make them our slaves; (3) have them convert to Islam and live with us in peace; or (4) collect taxes from them while they continue to practice their religion in secret.

"All over the world, these are the four choices," Sabaya continued. "This applies to you, too."

We sat there wondering why he was telling us this. We waited for some big announcement, but there was none. We were then dismissed.

A little while later, Reina was brought over for the same speech. Perhaps twenty or twenty-one years old, she was pretty and spunky. We watched her reading the same passages and listening to the same discourse.

But when she came back, she was visibly troubled. The speech had ended a little differently in her case. "He told me I have to be *sabaya*ed to one of these guys," she said, her voice shaking. "I have to live with him and sleep with him and everything."

"Oh, Reina!" we cried. "That's terrible!" We already knew she had a boyfriend back home in Lamitan.

"I know. I told him I'd rather be dead. But he said I had no option. So then I said, 'What's next?'

" 'Well, you get to choose which one you're going to go with,' he said."

What a predicament. We sat there staring into space, trying to figure out what she should do next. Was there any way to avoid this atrocity? We racked our brains and came up with nothing.

I finally said, "Well, Reina, what about Daud [David]? He seems noticeably kinder than the rest." Daud had lost his wife in childbirth several years before. He was new to the group and had a softer demeanor, not like some of the tougher types.

Reina just shook her head in disbelief at the whole predicament.

That evening, if it hadn't been so sad, it would have been comical to watch all of the Abu Sayyaf come "courting" Reina's interests. They brought cookies and candy and coffee; it turned into a regular party. They introduced themselves and wanted her to know as much about them as possible.

The next day, Reina was called again to talk with Sabaya. But when she returned, the deal had changed. "I don't get to choose after all," she reported to us with a heavy voice. "I've been given to Janjalani." No amount of protest would change the matter.

"He's the head guy," Sabaya had said, trying to make her feel better. "He's educated, and you'll be treated better with him than anyone else."

So in the end, that is what transpired. Reina dejectedly picked up her stuff and moved over the hill to Janjalani's hammock.

10
SURROUNDED

(Early July 2001)

WITH EVERY PASSING NIGHT we spent in the open, my bones seemed to hurt more. I was becoming an old lady at a rapid pace. I awoke in pain every hour or so and had to sit up, sometimes even stand. This disturbed Martin's sleep, of course, since we were routinely handcuffed together (now that Guillermo was gone), and the handcuff was then chained to a tree.

I thought to myself at one point, *Has there been even one night's sleep in captivity that I could honestly term "good"? Not really.*

One night just about dusk, some of the captors who had been out to get food came running back to our camp to report, "Soldiers! We've been 'confirmed.' They're going to raid us in the morning."

We pretended to go to bed that night, then got up again after dark and packed. Walking along the river in the black of night, our group of forty or fifty came within just a few hundred meters of the soldiers' camp. We moved silently past them and into the darkness.

While mobiling, we each had our own guard who was assigned to watch us and make sure we didn't try to escape. My guard was Sakaki, a pleasant enough fellow who seemed like he would have been more comfortable in the city than fighting as a tough guerrilla. On this particular trek, I was having a lot of trouble seeing in the dark because of night-vision problems that have plagued me ever since I had laser eye surgery. I couldn't see where I was going, and we were now walking *through* a river on big rocks. Seeing my struggle to keep up, Hurayra was assigned to help me instead of Sakaki.

For some reason, Hurayra carried a sniper rifle instead of an M16 like everyone else. But he could be kind when he wanted to. All through the jungle are leaves that are fluorescent; they actually glow at night from a mold of some kind. Hurayra picked up a handful of these and hooked them onto his backpack so I could follow him. After he climbed over a rock, he extended his hand to help me up. This was rare; most of the others refused to touch a woman, especially an American woman. (Some, when required to help me, actually wrapped towels around their hands so as to avoid contact.)

Hurayra's kindness extended to Martin as well; he called him "sir." At one point he started showing up every morning between eight and nine with "a gift for Mr. Martin"—coffee or cookies or maybe hot milk. He would sit with a little notebook and ask us to help him learn English.

"What do you call such and such?" he would ask, and Martin would answer.

They would work together for at least an hour and sometimes longer. He would ask all about the United States. His real goal, he explained, was to get to Afghanistan and die in holy war so he could go straight to paradise.

One day Hurayra wanted to learn the English word for defecation.

"Well, in our culture we don't really get that specific," I replied. "We just say, 'I have to go to the bathroom,' or 'I have to go to the CR.' It's considered crude to go into detail about exactly what you're going to do there."

He looked at us for a long time and then said, "If you only tell me you're going to the CR, I have many questions!"

I broke up laughing as I said, "Hurayra, if you see me heading out into the woods with my water jug and a *bolo* knife to dig a hole, you can figure it out, right? But I'm still only going to say, 'I'm going to the CR.'"

"Oh, okay . . . but I still have many questions!"

On another occasion while Martin and I were bathing at a little spring, Hurayra even volunteered to do our laundry for us. He seemed to understand that we were struggling to adjust to hostage life and needed to be helped along. He was just so polite and nice—for a terrorist!

Even though Reina was forced to spend most of her time with Janjalani now, we still tried to talk as often as we could. When we weren't mobiling, she and I had even more time together. She was understandably depressed about her new lot in life as Janjalani's mistress. But her natural spunk seemed to shine through, regardless.

Every once in a while, she would rise up and give Janjalani a piece of her mind. It was fun to listen. When he would say, "Look at all the support our movement has," she would fire back, "Well, sure the civilians support you—you've got money! You send them to town with 3,000 pesos [$60], and they bring you back one sack of rice and some dried fish—and they get to keep the rest. Wait till your money runs out."

Lalaine, on the other hand, seemed to be quite taken with Bro, who had been assigned as her bodyguard. This might have been a case of Stockholm syndrome, a reaction common in kidnapping situations, in which a hostage becomes sympathetic to or even falls in love with his or her captor. In any case, I knew she was in danger. "Lalaine, you need to be careful," I told the young teenager. "Remember, this guy's a terrorist."

"What?" she replied. "They've never done anything bad to me. They just want their homeland back."

"Lalaine, think a minute!" I said, quickly turning into a scolding aunt. "They forcibly took you away from a resort where you were vacationing with your family. Right now your parents are possibly selling their house in order to raise 10 million pesos for your freedom. They're probably pleading with everyone they know, going into debt to ransom you out of here. And you say these guys have never done anything to you? Lalaine, you've got to keep clear in your mind who the bad guys are."

"Well, at least they're not like the armed forces, who are just out here for the pay," she tried to reason.

"A country has to have armed forces, or else it won't survive," I countered. "These bandits would be totally out of control otherwise."

I don't know that I totally convinced her. The Abu Sayyaf had fed her a lot of propaganda. Fortunately, her ransom came through along with Chito's not much later, and the two of them were allowed to leave. Before they left, we urged Chito to call our children. I especially hated to see Lalaine leave; I had really grown to love her.

I was tempted to send out my wedding ring, which was still safely hidden in my pocket after all these weeks. But I held back, thinking that we'd probably be released ourselves before too long. After all, others were getting to go; we would surely get our opening soon, wouldn't we?

Chito's last words to Martin and me were, "Give me two weeks—a month at the most—and I'll have you out of here." That was July 3, 2001.

• • •

The motorbike that picked up Lalaine and Chito that night must have brought food, because after we walked for about an hour, we stopped in a deserted village to make a meal. The guys built a fire and we ate, even though it was two o'clock in the morning. By this time, we had learned to eat whenever food was available, regardless of what the clock said.

Actually, our food supply had been pretty good lately. We'd been eating about two meals each day, and even when we ran short, we could always resort to *pacō*, a dark green fern that grows in the jungle. We could snip off the curly tops and eat them raw. Since they're bright green, I assume they're quite healthy.

Sometimes the captors boiled the *pacó*. Other times they stir-fried it with a bit of onion. It was really very good.

Although they were still on a mission, the Abu Sayyaf didn't seem to be in an aggressive mode these days. They weren't pressing the battle against the AFP but were instead trying to avoid them, since they had to take care of us while waiting for their financial windfall.

This passivity was actually harder for these warriors than the gun battles were. They sometimes referred to their daily lot as "babysitting." Had it not been for us, they could have gone after the AFP with a vengeance.

At times, from up on a hill, we would spot an AFP camp. One of the guys would say to another, "Boy, if we didn't have these people, we'd go down there and raid them good!"

But the money was always thought to be "right around the corner," so we waited.

Somehow, the three of us—Joel, Martin, and I—ended up with a group of a dozen or so captors led by Mang Ben. We learned that as long as we were in Mang Ben's group, the goat meat would be extra spicy.

For some reason, he liked the idea of Hurayra learning English. He told the others in his group, "You need to do the same. You won't go far in this world without it."

Mang Ben organized his men into two-hour guard shifts throughout the night, to make sure we didn't escape. One night when I was sitting up to work the kinks out of my joints, Mang Ben's stern voice came booming out of the darkness:

"Why you do that?!"

I couldn't see his face at all. "Do what?" I asked in return.

"You lay down!" he ordered from his hammock.

"I'm sore; I hurt, because I'm lying on the ground." I continued to sit there for a while, despite his command. Eventually, however, I did lie down again to try to rest.

Honestly, the Abu Sayyaf really didn't need to worry about our trying to escape. Martin and I talked about the possibility all the time, but every time, we came to the same conclusion: If we tried to escape and were caught, we would be shot, end of story.

I know that if I hadn't been there, Martin would have escaped. In fact, he often told me that if ever I had the chance to get away, I should take it. "If I know you're out, I'll get away, too. Don't worry about me," he said. But he knew it would be impossible for us to escape together. Whenever we talked about it, he'd ask me, "How far can you run? If we leave together, they'll be after us in no time. These guys can run all day. Can you do that?" I'd have to admit that no, I couldn't.

"Gracia, my gut feeling is this: We're going to get out of here sooner or later," he'd say. "Believe me, I don't plan to make a career of this hostage thing."

And so we waited for our ransom money to arrive.

• • •

People in America often ask me if the Abu Sayyaf were cruel to me personally. Well, yes, of course—the whole kidnapping was cruel. But one incident stands out in my memory. I was suffering from diarrhea (a common condition for me). When Haija, an especially harsh captor, came one evening to chain Martin and me together, I knew I'd need to be up during the night. "I'm sick," I explained. "Would you please not chain me tonight?"

Without a word, he began securing us to each other and then to the tree.

"I'm going to have to go to the CR during the night," I said. "Please? I promise I'll be here in the morning. You know I won't leave Martin."

His handsome face remained a stone. He snapped the lock shut and handed the key to Sakaki, giving instructions in a language I didn't understand.

Guess I'll just have to bother Sakaki then, I thought to myself.

Not long into the night, I knew I needed to get up. "Sakaki! Sakaki!" I called. But I couldn't wake him.

Joel was sleeping nearby, and he heard my calls.

"Joel! Please go get the key from Sakaki!"

He sat up but didn't move farther. Instead, he started to rearrange and smooth the empty rice sacks on which we were sleeping.

"Joel—I have LBM [loose bowel movement]. I have to go into the woods!"

He still didn't answer but kept looking down at the rice sacks.

"What's wrong, Joel?"

Finally he spoke. "Haija said we're not allowed to let you free," he quietly admitted.

I started to panic. "Joel, what am I going to do?"

"I don't know."

Martin was still asleep. I looked around in growing desperation. I realized I had a plastic bag, left over from a bunch of bananas. So I gingerly slid over to one side, away from the others, squatted down, and used the bag as best I could there in the darkness. I felt utterly degraded. Any source of water for cleaning up was, of course, beyond my reach.

To me, that qualified as cruelty.

Early the next morning, as the sun was just coming up and before we were unchained, Joel was thoughtful enough to remove the bag into the woods. That day, we raised a healthy complaint about all this to Solaiman. We told him how awful it had been. He didn't apologize, but after that our treatment seemed to improve a bit.

Every so often, we'd make a wish list of things we needed. For example, on one such list, I put deodorant, two apples, two oranges, and peanut butter. We got the deodorant and peanut butter (a new food experience for the Abu Sayyaf). We also ended up with two big packages of Apple Dapple cookies (seventy-two in all) and two packages of orange crème cookies (again, a total of seventy-two)!

This was great for Martin and me, because Muslims refuse to

eat anything that contains MSG or shortening. That meant we got the cookies all to ourselves.

My mosquito bites had gotten infected, and I didn't have enough self-control not to scratch them. One day I said to Martin, "If I could wish for anything right now, it would be a bottle of rubbing alcohol."

Not more than thirty minutes later, one of the guys walked by and tossed us a bottle of Green Cross rubbing alcohol. "From Solaiman," he said, and kept walking. Of all the random things!

One of the captors was the cutest seventeen-year-old named Ibno Sahid. He often perched his hammock directly over us. Whenever we said something to him, he got the biggest smile on his face.

Then I realized that he didn't speak a lick of English. He just knew when to smile and nod.

Eventually, he came to me, with Joel as his interpreter. "I want to learn to read," he said, explaining that he didn't know how to read any language at all.

"Well, you get a notebook like Hurayra's," I replied. "Get a pen, too, and I'll start teaching you English."

He found a little spiral notebook, and for our first lesson, I wrote his name on the opening page. I showed him an empty peanut butter jar and then wrote down the words "peanut butter." I also began teaching him what the different letters sounded like.

I figured it wouldn't hurt to be helpful to a young guy like this. And it gave me something to do with my mind other than worry about things outside my control.

• • •

One day, some planes flew over in a pattern. "What are those?" the Abu Sayyaf asked Martin, knowing that he was informed about such things.

"Those planes are searching for us," Martin replied. We all grew a bit more nervous. Soon the order came to pack up again for moving out. But then we sat and waited for firm instructions while the leaders huddled together. They delayed so long that a couple of the guys put their hammocks back up again. I sat talking with Reina, and we began to relax.

All of a sudden, across an open field, we saw soldiers heading straight for us. The guns blazed, and we all dropped to the ground.

"Reina! Come with us!" I said.

"No, no—I have to go back to the emir," she answered, using the Arabic term for "leader." She headed one direction back toward Janjalani, while we headed the other way. We ran, then dropped, then ran, then dropped again.

As soon as we were able to regroup, we saw that Ibno had been wounded quite badly, along with two other captors. Reina had gotten some shrapnel in her face. The battle quieted down, and we walked about fifteen minutes down toward a river. Suddenly, gunfire opened up right ahead of us. We dropped and ran once again.

Joel landed right beside me at one point, and in his terror, I think he was praying every prayer he'd ever heard. First it was "Holy Mary, Mother of God, pray for us sinners both now and at the hour of our death." Soon, however, he switched to *"Allah akbar! Allah akbar! Allah akbar!"*

"Pray, Gracia, pray!" he urged.

"I'm praying, Joel, I'm praying!" I guess he thought because he didn't hear me verbally, I must not be doing my part.

A helicopter appeared overhead, searching for us. We huddled under trees in order to stay out of sight. In the midst of this danger, however, I looked up—and there was Bro using one of the stolen video cameras from Dos Palmas, filming the whole scene! *This man is absolutely fearless,* I thought.

The helicopter eventually flew away, and we tried to hike again—until we ran into yet another group of AFP soldiers. We realized we were trapped in the field. We had no choice but to sit down in the hot sun and wait.

There was a stream of water in that field, but it was full of leech eggs. We had to drink something in order to stay hydrated in the hot sun, so we closed our eyes and gulped it down.

Then out of nowhere, a bag of ripe *lansones* started going down the line of captors and hostages. Where they came from I have no idea. I absolutely love *lansones*—they're a fruit a little smaller than an apricot and sort of like a grape inside.

"Gracia, it's your favorite fruit!" Martin said.

"Yes, it is!"

"Can you believe it? Right here in the middle of this battle, the Lord managed to get you some *lansones*!" Martin said with a chuckle.

Around four that afternoon, I was off in the weeds when Sakaki began yelling, "Ma'am! ma'am! Come, come, come!" I got back to him just as the gunfire broke out again. This battle simply would not quit.

We crawled on our elbows until we got into a group again. While we were lying there, someone arrived with stunning news.

Mang Ben had been killed.

I stared off into space, thinking of his wife and three children back home—a boy, a girl, and then another boy—just like our family. I began to cry quietly. This man, our group's leader, was already at that moment plunging into an eternity he wasn't ready for.

I thought about the reason Martin and I had come to the Philippines in the first place: to help people like Mang Ben find forgiveness through Christ and get ready for the hereafter. The tears now came harder than ever.

The only way I was able to regain my composure was to remember that this is what Mang Ben had always said he wanted: to die in jihad. He had gotten his wish after all.

Suddenly, Hurayra bolted down toward the stream with bullets still whizzing by. As he ran, he screamed at the top of his lungs, "Fifty-seven! Fifty-seven!"

The AFP thought that an M57—a bazooka that could do a lot of damage—was being loaded up to fire at them, and they scattered in retreat. This gave the Abu Sayyaf time to drag Mang Ben's body back to the group.

I stayed in the grass, lying facedown. It was so unbelievably hot, I began to hyperventilate. I looked over at the wounded Ibno, who was breathing heavily. It didn't seem as though his injuries were serious enough to be fatal, but I still felt so badly for him. My mind began to cloud over, the same sensation I'd felt back in the hospital corridor in Lamitan when we were being bombed. My brain seemed to be shutting down. I fought to get my breath.

"I'm just going to sleep," I murmured to Martin, who was lying close to me.

"Okay," he answered.

I laid my head down and actually drifted off for a few minutes.

My repose was broken, however, by a swirl of animated talk about what to do with Mang Ben's body. If the AFP got their hands on it, they could turn it in for a reward of several thousand pesos. The Abu Sayyaf were determined not to let them have that satisfaction.

By then it was dark, and they carried the body to the far end of the field. Someone used the sat-phone to call Mang Ben's village and tell them to come get their fallen brother.

That night, Mang Ben's gear was brought into camp for dispersing. I ended up with a backpack—not Mang Ben's, because it was too nice. But the person who got that backpack gave his old one to someone else, and so on down the line, until eventually I ended up with a shabby one. At least it was a place for my things. I happily began loading up my sheet, deodorant, some sanitary napkins I'd been able to acquire, and the precious Burnham toothbrush.

Amazingly, we were able to walk out of that area under cover of darkness. I couldn't believe it. Just as at the hospital, the government troops didn't seem interested in pursuing us. After all, it was night now; their "shift" was over. Their commitment to the cause certainly had its limits—unlike that of the Muslim rebels, who would fight to the death for the reward of instant paradise (with its seventy-two dark-eyed perpetual virgins waiting).

We mobiled all night. Our three casualties were carried in *malongs* by the others. Then Ibno's older brother came along, leading a *carabao* (water buffalo). The water buffalo was pulling a rig with a huge woven basket, and we could use it to carry our wounded. Where he had commandeered it I could only guess.

Some new faces joined us, from where I didn't know; perhaps they were from Mang Ben's village. They followed at the end of the column as we moved along the trail.

Every hour or so, we stopped for a short rest. I usually used these stops to head out into the brush for another bathroom break.

At one such place, I left my backpack beside Martin, and when I returned, everyone was already standing up to walk again. I quickly fell in line behind Martin, who was tied to Sakaki ahead of him. I had an odd feeling of lightness. *I've just been through another gun battle, and we're not getting any sleep tonight—but I still feel so light, almost like I'm bouncing along here,* I thought.

Suddenly it hit me: I didn't have my backpack! No wonder.

I immediately turned around to retrace my steps the hundred yards or so and get it.

"No!" one of the new guys barked at me. "You go!"

"Oh, please, my backpack's there, with all my things!" I pleaded. "It's just a little way. Let me get it, please, and I'll catch up."

He cocked his gun at me as he repeated, "No—you go!"

I didn't know this fellow at all. If he had been one of the familiar captors, I would have ignored him and gone back up the trail anyway. But this one seemed so callous. Did I dare challenge him?

I turned around to run forward and catch Sakaki. I pleaded, "Sakaki, my backpack! I left it back there; help me!"

He tried to intercede on my behalf, but before he could get out half a sentence, the new guard cut him off. "No—you go! Hurry!"

My heart sank to the bottom of my toes. Everything we owned in this life was back there in that backpack. The sheet we pulled over us at night, my long-sleeved shirt, our toothbrush—it was all there. A horrible wave of guilt swept over me. *How stupid of me! I just lost it all.*

"Oh, Martin, I'm so sorry, I'm so sorry!" I cried between my sobs.

My husband did not reproach me. He just quietly answered, "You know, honey, we've got to save our energy for walking. I forgive you. And you need to forgive yourself. It's going to be okay."

But I couldn't forgive myself. I was engulfed in torment. There was nothing I could do now to correct my tragic mistake. I had to keep putting one foot in front of the other the rest of that night. With every step, I mourned.

11
A SONG FOR THE JUNGLE

(Late July 2001)

AROUND DAYBREAK, we arrived utterly exhausted in a small village. In fact, our single-file column was disintegrating as various people slumped down and instantly fell asleep, only to be roused by others to keep going.

A small shelter came into view. As we got closer, we saw a welcome sight: some ripe bananas on the ground. Suddenly energized, I ran to grab as many as I could, even stuffing some into my pockets for later. Martin and I sat on the ground and savored every bite of nourishment.

The people of that village must have felt very safe, because they openly came around to sit with us and talk in their language. They looked at our wounded and made clucking sounds of sympathy. They arranged for Ibno and the other two wounded men to be evacuated on a boat to Zamboanga, where they could get medical attention.

And then, who should show up in the middle of this small village but Sakaki's wife! As a Muslim woman, she was totally covered from head to toe with the black garb; I couldn't even see her eyes through the netting. Her hands were covered with black cloth as well.

But to us, she might as well have been an angel in shining white, because she carried with her a big green bag for us with a long strap.

She handed it to Solaiman, who pawed through it, removing several items before he brought it over to Martin and me.

Inside were *malong*s and soap and toothpaste and sanitary napkins. As I sorted through the items, I realized the bag contained everything I had lost the night before! I gasped with joy. It was as if God had already planned ahead to erase my disastrous loss. Suddenly the tragedy of our horrible night on the trail was reversed. But the bag contained an even greater treasure: letters for us! They were our first contact from loved ones after two months on the run. How in the world had she received these? We had no idea, but we didn't care. We were just grateful to hear from our children.

Jeff's letter said:

Hey my cool parents,
　　We are having fun here with Grandma and Grandpa and all our cousins. Aunt Felicia took us to rent movies just now. It was great. I didn't really enjoy the movie we got but that's okay. I just wanted to say hi and that I'm looking forward to seeing you again. I'm praying for you. Bye.
　　Jeff (the cool one)

He then added a happy face. I don't think Martin and I had smiled this broadly in weeks. What a thrill to hear from our firstborn.

Mindy wrote about going to the animal clinic and all the dogs and cats she had seen. She concluded by saying,

I just want you to know I am praying for you. Bye Mom, bye Dad.
　　Love always, Mindy
　　P.S. Happy Fathers Day dad.

It was so sweet.

Ten-year-old Zach's was short and to the point.

Dear Mom and Dad,
How are you? I am fine. We went to Walmart today. It is fun
here. At Mega Mall we bought two computer games.
I will write you back.
Love, Zach

We just screeched with delight, laughing especially about his last line about writing us back. "No! We don't want to be here long enough to get another letter from Zach!" we said. We wanted instead to go running into that house in Rose Hill, Kansas, and sweep that little guy into our arms for a long, long hug.

There were letters from Martin's parents, my parents, each of Martin's siblings, and others as well. We sat reading them aloud to each other again and again. Some of the letters had pictures. We gleefully showed them around.

And finally, the bag contained a pair of replacement glasses for Martin. We figured that Francis or Chito must have called our New Tribes Mission colleagues and explained Martin's need. So here was a new pair of his prescription from the same optical provider in Manila's sprawling Mega Mall.

"I can tell what these people look like now!" Martin exclaimed to me, a big smile on his face. For nearly two months he had been living in a haze.

The dear woman had also brought along a second big bag of bread rolls. The Abu Sayyaf looked at them but were skeptical about the ingredients. So Joel, Martin, and I had a whole bag of bread to eat. We dove right in.

I went over to Sakaki's wife and gave her a big hug. "Thank you so much for coming," I said. "Sakaki is a good guard."

She nodded, and we talked briefly. She told me she was an elementary schoolteacher.

A while later, Fatima, who fancied himself one of the religious leaders of the Abu Sayyaf, called over.

"Hey, Martin, let me see your new glasses."

"Why?" Martin asked him.

"I just want to see them."

Martin took them to Fatima. The man held them in his hand, turning them one way and then another as he studied them. Then he announced without warning: "We'll keep these. If you had them, they would help you escape."

No! I wanted to scream, or jump up and dig my fingernails into Fatima's flesh. Martin was finally enjoying clear vision after all this time. We stared at the man. Martin's shoulders sagged with disappointment. Finally, he said, "Well, you might as well have the case, too. I don't want them getting messed up, in case I can ever have them back."

Fatima took the case, saying, "Yes, maybe someday." He passed the glasses along to Haija, who put them in his backpack.

We never saw those glasses again. Martin had worn them for less than two hours.

• • •

Sakaki, of course, was delighted to see his wife. He asked if he could have a one-night leave with her. He'd be back in the morning, he promised. Permission was granted.

After he left, the others noticed that Sakaki had taken his gun with him. Everyone got upset—especially Zacarias. After all, why did he need his weapon to go home for a visit? Some of the other Abu Sayyaf had no guns at all.

The villagers volunteered to kill a cow and throw a feast for us. The meat was being cooked in pots over an open fire, and delicious smells began to waft through the air. My mouth was watering as I imagined what that fresh beef was going to taste like. We hadn't had beef since . . .

"*Sundalo!* At the school! Everybody pack up!" There would be no feast after all.

We did manage to collect some of the pots and the half-cooked meat to carry with us up the hill and into the woods. Martin proudly carried the new green bag with all our goodies.

Curiously, we never saw Sakaki again. His overnight leave request turned out to be a permanent defection from the Abu Sayyaf.

This left Martin and me without an official guard, so Hurayra was appointed to take on this responsibility. This was nice for us, because Hurayra had such a gentle spirit.

A brand-new recruit from the village joined us in our trek. His English was quite good. Although I never did catch his name, I remember him because of something he said while we were sitting on top of the hill. Wearing only a T-shirt, shorts, and *tsinelas,* he said with uncommon frankness, "I never wanted to be a soldier. I never wanted to be in jihad. But these guys said they needed me."

It was a brief but poignant testimony to the fact that coercion was not just a tactic for hostages. It was apparently standard practice throughout the Abu Sayyaf.

Later that day, Sabaya came over to where Martin and I were sitting. "They're asking for a 'proof of life,'" he told us.

"Who's 'they'?"

"We're not sure."

But then later, Solaiman appeared to know more. "It's that guy who's always smoking a cigar on TV," he volunteered, referring to the trademark pose of former Philippine president Fidel Ramos.

Soon Martin and I were ushered in front of a camera. Sabaya had assumed his beloved hard-guy image: dark sunglasses, knit cap, weapon in hand. Bro took the shots. Then the film was removed from the camera, and Sabaya told him where to deliver it in town.

They also asked us to make a tape recording. Martin was told what to say, of course: "Please bring this matter to a swift end. Please appoint a mediator."

Next, I was asked to record something for President Arroyo— sort of "mother to mother," they said. So I put together a little speech, pleading with her as a woman to work something out with this group, because I really wanted to see my children again. "Please do whatever you can, and have mercy on us," I concluded.

This tape was sent out along with the photo film.

As we walked away, I found myself coming to terms with the thought that this captivity just might be a long thing after all. Others had been ransomed—Reggie and Rizza, Francis and Tess, Letty and Kim and Lalaine, even Chito—but no such hope existed for us. The days were going on, there was always another trail to hike, another hill to climb . . . this wasn't going to end anytime soon. I began to be depressed.

In the days that followed, the depression really took hold. I thought about all that Jeff and Mindy and Zach must be going through without me, and the tears started to flow. A pall settled in around me and I just sat and cried, which was new for me. I had never been the weepy type—until now. The captors hated to see me crying. I tried to be quiet about it, and I hated to have Martin see me in this state. He had known me for many years and he knew I wasn't the type of person to be sad or upset for long. He was especially concerned and did his best to lift my spirits. But I just couldn't seem to snap out of it.

I didn't see Reina at all during our stay on that mountaintop. The poor girl had been through an awful ordeal with her face wound. She asked Joel to clean out the shrapnel, and he tried. But with no anesthesia, the pain was just too great. Finally, she took the forceps from the medical bag, got a mirror, gritted her teeth, and did the job herself.

It turned out not to be shrapnel after all. It was a splinter from a tree that had been shredded by a mortar during the all-day battle.

• • •

Sabaya came to Martin one day and said, "You've told us you were never in the armed forces. Did you lie to us?"

"No, I didn't," he replied. "I got out of college and went right into mission work."

"Then why is Fidel Ramos calling you a 'brother'?"

"I don't know," Martin replied with puzzlement.

"Well, you must have been in the army with him!"

Martin thought for a moment and said, "Actually, for one thing, I'm a lot younger than Fidel Ramos. If he called anyone 'brother,' it would more likely be someone the age of my dad, who was a paratrooper in the army, for whatever that's worth."

The interrogation continued. "Tell us why he's using that term for you," they insisted again.

"It's my understanding that Fidel Ramos is a Protestant," Martin suggested next. "Maybe that's what he means; we're 'brothers in the faith.'"

"Oh, that must be it," they concluded. We both relaxed. The Abu Sayyaf were in fact encouraged by this bit of news and thought the negotiation stood a better chance as a result.

Not too long after this conversation, they announced, "We're going to take you back to rejoin the other hostage group."

Thus began a several-day walk. As always, Martin was tied with a rope to one of the captors while walking. And, as before, we were both chained to a tree at night. One morning as we were up building fires to ward off the cold, Solaiman called us over and said, "Your kids are going to speak on the radio here in just a minute." We quickly huddled around the battery-powered radio, which was tuned as usual to Radyo Agong.

Sure enough, we heard their voices!

"Hello, this is Jeff Burnham, the oldest son of Martin and Gracia Burnham. I just want to ask the Abu Sayyaf not to hurt my parents. They really weren't doing anything wrong when they went to that resort for their anniversary. There's no reason to harm them. Mom and Dad, I'm doing okay. I love you."

Then came Mindy. She introduced herself and again gave a message directly to the Abu Sayyaf, similar to Jeff's.

Even young Zach did a good job. As his mother, I could tell that he didn't really want to be making a speech, but he carried through for our sakes.

We were so happy. To hear their voices was an unbelievable treat and dispelled the chill from our hearts.

Meanwhile, Solaiman looked at Martin and me with amazement. "Those kids are talking to us!"

"Yes, they are. They don't want you to hurt us."

I sensed just a hint of softness in that moment. After all, he was a father too, with kids at home. Filipinos love their families very deeply. I think his heart was touched.

• • •

Finally, we arrived at our destination, which turned out to be House 125. I was disappointed when I saw it, because it meant we were just going in circles, wearing ourselves out for no purpose. The striking force that had left us six weeks before was waiting for us. Sure enough, there was no Guillermo Sobero. The force had gathered a crop of new hostages: thirteen boys, some as young as thirteen years old, from a coconut plantation called Golden Harvest. Two others had tried to run away and been shot to death, they said. All the others had supposedly converted to Islam.

This was our first clue of things to come.

The house had been thoroughly trashed in our absence. Junk was everywhere and the place was filthy. I found an old rag in the corner and brushed the debris out of the room where we would be sleeping.

But as it turned out, we didn't stay there after all. Near the end of that day, we were put back on the trail again, destination unknown as always. The Abu Sayyaf were especially concerned that we not leave footprints, even when we came upon a stash of sugarcane that some of the guys very much wanted. We hiked all that night, and toward dawn, we arrived at a camp.

To reach this camp, which was along a beautiful river, we had to descend a steep cliff. This was the toughest terrain we had dealt with yet. At one point I lost my footing and went sliding toward the edge. At the last second, I caught a tree.

Hanging down over an expanse below, I managed to climb back up the trunk. We continued inching downward. At the water's edge, we began moving from one rock to another in the river for a while, then up a hill, finally arriving at the camp, which belonged to the MILF (Moro Islamic Liberation Front). Their dialogue with the government was going better than the Abu Sayyaf's, we learned. They had recently been granted amnesty for past episodes.

By this point, we were all exhausted. My littlest toes were absolutely ruined. I could barely hobble along.

We found ourselves directed in the darkness toward a thatched-roof house about eight feet square, with a porch of equal size. Once inside, we were shocked to find Angie, Fe, Ediborah, and Sheila waiting there to greet us! What a reunion that was. We hugged each other and all jabbered at once, thanking God that we were back together again.

"Why do you think our two groups have been brought back together?" I asked.

"Well, someone in Malaysia is negotiating a release," one of the girls said. "They want to release us all together."

That sounded great to us, of course. We told the girls about all our adventures, the battle in the field, how hard we'd hiked, and how we'd been starving a lot of the time. Then they told us their side of the story—that they had been taken to a really nice location and sat for three or four weeks, with plenty to eat and no soldiers nearby. It made for quite a contrast.

"Reina—where's Reina?" they wanted to know.

"Well, she's with Janjalani," I reported.

"Oh. So it's true—she's been *sabaya*ed. We didn't believe that would happen."

Reina, who shared a house with Janjalani, was in fact ashamed to come over and talk to the others for several days.

After some more catching up, I turned to Fe and Angie to do what I knew must be done. "This is going to be hard for you to hear," I began, "but I feel like you need to know. I don't know what you have been told, but we've been told that Guillermo is dead."

"No, no one told us!" said Fe, her eyes starting to cloud up.

"Well, they did tell," Angie admitted, "but I didn't think I should say anything."

Fe stopped for a moment, then said with tenderness, "He's not really dead. He's alive in my heart. I won't ever forget him."

She wanted details about his death, of course, but I didn't have any.

Hardly a day later, however, Haija bluntly informed her that he had been the executioner. He spared no feelings. "It would have been harder for me to kill a dog than to kill Guillermo," he announced with some satisfaction. "He was a bad guy."

Fe was furious, of course. "What right does he have to judge Guillermo?" she stormed. None of us knew quite what to say. We just tried to comfort her as best we could.

. . .

We were informed that Sheila and Ediborah had converted to Islam during their time away from us. Apparently, they had been told that if they converted, they would be released. So they had done all the prayers to become Muslims.

To their great disappointment, they didn't get released after all, but their daily treatment began to show a marked improvement. They were given more to eat, and they received a more steady supply of deodorant, shampoo, and other amenities. Omar, the leader of their group, also seemed to be showing a personal interest in Sheila, so he was especially looking out for her welfare.

All of this, understandably, did not sit well with Angie, who held to her Catholic faith, and Fe, who was Mormon.

"There are six of us here, but only four of us are hostages," Angie complained to me one day, speaking of the six of us in the house.

"Well, Sheila and Ediborah are still hostages," I replied. "They obviously can't leave. Angie, we all need to stick together; we can't afford to be at odds with one another. We've got to live in this little tiny hut."

"We're already at odds," said Angie. "Fe and I think that at night, you and Martin should sleep in the middle, and the two of us can sleep on one side of you, while the two of them sleep on the opposite side. That way we won't have to even be near each other."

But soon that plan was discarded, because the Abu Sayyaf weren't going to let a man sleep beside a woman who wasn't his wife. So they put Martin tight up against a wall, then me, then Angie and Fe, followed by a wide space, with Ediborah and Sheila against the opposite wall. Again, I found myself pushing all night long trying to get a decent amount of room.

As time went on without proper sleep, my emotional state continued to deteriorate. It was our tenth week in captivity, the time I had set in my own mind for our release back on the speedboat. *Worst-case scenario, we'll spend the summer with these guys and be out by the time the kids go back to school,* I had told myself. Now August was nearly here, and I could see no hope for progress. The feelings of despair were overwhelming.

I often found myself sitting on a rock by the river, staring at leaves caught between rocks in the water. Whenever a leaf would break free and start floating down the river, I would be happy for that leaf. I'd just sit there and watch it, wishing I could go down the river with it and be free.

In the constant rumble of the river, it was like I could hear Satan laughing at me, saying, "You trust in the Lord—but you're still here." I found myself beginning to believe Satan's lies.

netimes Martin would come and sit with me by the river. He'd say, "I just hate to see you giving up your faith like this."

"Oh, I'm not giving up my faith," I'd tell him. "I still believe that God made the world, he sent his Son, Jesus, and Jesus died for me. I haven't given up my faith—I'm just choosing not to believe the part about God loving me. Because God's not coming through."

"It seems to me that either you believe it all, or else you don't believe at all," was Martin's gentle reply.

Music had always been such a big part of my life; I sang softly to myself all the time. Now, I found that I could still sing songs like "I Sing the Mighty Power of God" and other majestic anthems. But I refused to sing "O Love That Will Not Let Me Go." I was really mad at God.

After about three days of living with this torment, I was totally miserable. When I wasn't at the river crying, I was in the house crying. Finally, Martin learned not to say anything, because he knew this was something I had to work through myself.

One day as I was sitting at the river, I thought about some of the things Martin had said. I realized that my depression and anger against God weren't doing anything to make our situation more bearable. In fact, they were only making it worse—for me as well as for everyone around me. I knew that I had a choice. I could give in to my resentment and allow it to dig me into a deeper and deeper hole both psychologically and emotionally, or I could choose to believe what God's Word says to be true whether I felt it was or not.

This was a turning point for me. It was as if God were saying to me, "If you're going to believe that I died for you, why not believe that I love you? Why don't you let me put my arms around you and love you?"

And I did. I simply gave in and handed all my pain and anger over to the Lord right then and there. I didn't have a Bible or anyone but Martin encouraging me. But from that day on, the Lord somehow let me know in my spirit that he was still faithful.

• • •

Back at the cabin a day or so later, I apologized for the way I had been behaving and said that God and I had come to an agreement: He loved me and I was choosing to believe it.

Gradually, my singing increased. Fe knew some of the same hymns I knew and so we sang together. "How Great Thou Art" became our favorite. I'm sure the songwriter wasn't thinking of Basilan Island when he penned those words. But living in the jungle under the open sky, we could certainly identify with them. Angie didn't know the song, so we borrowed a pen and paper and wrote out these words for her:

> *O Lord my God! when I in awesome wonder*
> *Consider all the worlds*[†] *Thy hands have made,*
> *I see the stars, I hear the rolling*[†] *thunder,*
> *Thy power throughout the universe displayed.*
>
> *Then sings my soul, my Savior God, to Thee:*
> *How great Thou art! How great Thou art!*

The second and third verses expressed our circumstances even better:

> *When through the woods and forest glades I wander*
> *And hear the birds sing sweetly in the trees,*
> *When I look down from lofty mountain grandeur*
> *And hear the brook and feel the gentle breeze,*
>
> *And when I think that God, His Son not sparing,*
> *Sent Him to die, I scarce can take it in;*

† Author's original words are *works* and *mighty*.

That on the cross, my burden gladly bearing,
He bled and died to take away my sin.

Then sings my soul, my Savior God, to thee:
*How great Thou art! How great Thou art!**

Within a day, Angie knew the words by heart. I was able to harmonize with them, and we sounded quite good. We sang this song every day, sometimes several times a day.

The Abu Sayyaf never hissed at us for singing it. It sounded beautiful, and they liked music. More than once, Martin said to me, "Maybe God has us here just to praise him in this very dark place."

Gradually, my crisis of faith passed. I realized it would do no good to be angry with God. He had neither inspired the Abu Sayyaf to abduct us nor would he force them against their will to release us. Instead, he would sustain us day by day, night by night, mile by mile, for as long as it took.

Martin sometimes helped me get to sleep with his favorite hymn, "Wonderful Peace." He would hold my hand and quietly sing:

Far away in the depths of my spirit tonight
Rolls a melody sweeter than psalm;
In celestial-like strains it unceasingly falls
O'er my soul like an infinite calm.

Peace, peace, wonderful peace,
Coming down from the Father above!
Sweep over my spirit forever, I pray,
In fathomless billows of love!

And in that divine peace, I could rest.

12
JUSTICE OR MERCY?
(August–Early September 2001)

THROUGHOUT OUR CAPTIVITY, our days ran to one of two extremes, it seemed. Either we were mobiling to the point of exhaustion, running for our lives . . . or else we were sitting with absolutely nothing to do, bored stiff. The weeks in the MILF camp along the river were definitely the second of the two.

For some reason, our little shack became the place for our captors to hang out and try to pass the hours. Way into the night, Abu Sayyaf members sat around on the porch just talking and laughing. We woke up each morning to the sight of wall-to-wall guys just lying around asleep.

By now, we were pretty familiar with our captors so I really didn't mind having them so close, except when they got out their Korans and started their required reading aloud. They used a nasal, singsong chant, and there could be twenty different mumbly melody lines going on at the same time—each person on a different passage. It got so grating I used to tell Martin, "I've just got to get away from the 'choir practice.'" I'd pick up my water jug and a *bolo* knife and pretend I was heading off to go to the bathroom, whether I needed to or not.

One of the guys, while reading the Koran, turned every few lines and spit. I started wondering if it was forbidden to swallow while reading the Koran!

Meanwhile, the rest of us were trying to figure out what we could do to stay entertained. We amused ourselves with contests to see how many flies we could catch with our hands. Martin usually won.

Sometimes we sat and watched the ants, who were always busy. We got a kick out of watching them move some pretty amazing loads.

Another insect that fascinated me was the water strider. I loved to watch them walking across long distances of still water—I could never figure out how they did that. They always seemed like such cheerful insects.

At times I told myself we were getting downright lazy. I'd look at Martin and say, "Do you want to brush your teeth now?" And he'd say, "Nope. I'm just going to sit here." It was pretty pathetic when the most exciting part of our day was deciding whether or not to brush our teeth.

Angie and Fe and I sometimes braided each other's hair. One day I said to Fe, "Would you like a back rub?"

"No," she replied.

Later, I posed the same question to Angie.

"Sure." So I started rubbing her back.

Soon Fe was interested after all. "Is that what a back rub is? Yeah, I want one of those!" So we added back rubs to our list of things to do.

In the absence of any grooming tools, I learned to pluck my eyebrows and chin hairs with my fingers. It sounds hard, but it can be done. I simply pinched the hair between my forefinger and thumbnail as hard as I could, then jerked.

It was even tougher to take care of my fingernails and toenails with no clipper or nail file. Actually, my preferred method

---

August 7
The Philippine government signs a cease-fire with the Moro Islamic Liberation Front (MILF) but continues to stonewall the Abu Sayyaf.

for fingernails was to chew them off, but of course my hands were almost always dirty, and Martin said, "Don't chew your nails!" The only other option was to let my nails grow out to a certain length, then get them as moist and soft as possible in the river, and *carefully* tear off the top edge.

Toenails, we found, were far more treacherous to tear than fingernails. One little slip, and we would be down into the quick. Ouch! Every step for the next few days was painful.

About this time I realized that my ears weren't pierced anymore. Weeks before, during a quick getaway, I had left my earrings lying on a windowsill. Now I found that the holes had closed up.

Whenever Martin's mustache grew long enough to be offensive by Muslim standards, we borrowed scissors from the guys. Martin was mostly bald but the back of his neck still needed to be kept clean. Several times we ordered razors so I could shave it for him. I'd already been his barber throughout the years, having learned that skill back in mission boot camp in order to save money. We actually kept him looking pretty good out there in the jungle.

Ordering supplies from the guys sent into town was always a hit-and-miss proposition. We never knew if they understood what we wanted, or whether they'd follow through. I giggled at the thought of sending these tough warriors out to bring back sanitary napkins, but I figured that was their problem rather than mine. That's what they got for holding women hostage, right?

Their main purpose in town, of course, was to buy food. The term they used for groceries was "budget" (in the sense of quota or allotment). When the meal was ready on the fire—rice and maybe something to go with it—they'd yell, "Budget, budget!" and we'd all run to the fire with our banana leaf or a plate or pot or whatever we had to hold our little portion. On other occasions, the captors brought the budget to us.

One time Martin cracked a joke by saying, "When we get out of here and back to Rose Hill, I'm going to have so much fun driving down to the IGA [supermarket] for the budget!"

By now, I was totally sick of rice. I like rice—but I'd never had to eat it morning, noon, and night, seven days a week. Often we had nothing to go on top of it, not even salt.

One day I threw a little fit. I told the other hostages, "I can't stand any more rice! Every time it comes, I'm so hungry and know I need to eat some—but I'm so sick of it."

The next morning I announced to Martin, "I'm going to skip my meal. I'll be at the river." I stayed there for a long time so I wouldn't even have to smell the rice.

When I came back to the cabin, Martin didn't say anything. But waiting there on my plate was a big round *apam*—the Muslim version of a pancake made from flour, water, and sugar! We had never received one of these before. In fact, I couldn't remember getting anything made with flour at all. I was totally humbled and felt awful for complaining. I prayed, *Thank you, Lord. You knew I truly couldn't handle any more rice, and you sent me a pancake!*

Fe and Angie, on the other hand, had their own ways of adding variety to their diet. I told them they had "sticky fingers," an English expression they found amusing. One evening, they went off and didn't return for a while. When they finally came back, they were laughing.

"We've just been over at Musab's fire, and as we were leaving in the dark, we stole these sardines!" They proudly showed four cans.

"You guys!" I exclaimed. "You're gonna get in big trouble!"

"No, no, people steal food all the time. We were just taking our share."

Soon after, when our rice was brought around, Martin was off talking to Solaiman for some reason. The three of us found something to pry open the cans and poured on the sardines in tomato sauce.

"Do you want to pray for the meal?" they asked. I agreed.

Throughout August
Jones family members want to raise public awareness but are persuaded by New Tribes Mission to keep quiet for the time being.

"O Lord, I thank you so much for these girls with 'sticky fingers,'" I prayed. Everybody burst out laughing.

Angie and Fe had another talent that I could never quite master. We called it *langaw*ing, from the Tagalog word for housefly. If, for example, you have some food, and others come swarming around saying, "Can I have a bite?" you're obligated to feed the *langaw*. It is not culturally acceptable to refuse.

These two girls were really good at *langaw*ing, while Martin and I couldn't bring ourselves to beg. Occasionally, I swallowed my pride and tried it, however—and often the person said no! After all, I was *(a)* not Filipino and *(b)* a woman, so they felt no cultural pressure to share with me.

Sometimes I got really tired of being viewed as incompetent and stupid—a lower life-form—all because I didn't *langaw*, know how to build a fire, or like going to the bathroom in the open.

When it got to be the right season for marang fruit, we all were happy. One of the boys climbed trees all over the place and brought back the fruit for us. Marang are green with spiky skin, and they hurt if you grasp them too hard. But if you stick your thumbs in at the right place, they kind of fall open. Inside is a gooey mass of little white pods, and in each little pod is a black seed. You stick each pod in your mouth and spit out the seed. What's left is wonderfully sweet.

I forgot to mention that when the guys went out for budget, they'd pick up ammunition as well. You may wonder how such a group as the Abu Sayyaf always seemed to be well supplied with weaponry. Were their al-Qaeda friends sending them supply boats in the middle of the night?

No, no—nothing so exotic as that. The Abu Sayyaf told us their source was none other than the Philippine army itself. More than once I heard Solaiman on the sat-phone calling Zamboanga, talking to a lady named Ma'am Blanco. He would give her all his specifications for guns, bullets, you name it.

"Who are you ordering from?" we asked him one day.

"Oh, the army," he replied. "We pay a lot more than it should cost, of course. So somebody's making a lot of money. But at least we get what we need."

I was amazed. The fact that such firepower could quite possibly wind up killing one's fellow soldiers seemed not to matter at all.

•   •   •

Solaiman was just as bored as we were, so he had ample time for theological discussions. He really wanted us to understand Islam as a religion of justice.

"We are trying to get justice for everything bad that has ever happened to us," he explained. He recited all the atrocities against Muslims starting back before the Crusades and explained how they were seeking retribution.

He talked about how awful the Philippine army had been to Muslims. Years ago, he claimed, the government couldn't get control of the southern Philippines because Muslims were such fierce warriors, so they sent down Christians (his term) to colonize the area. They eventually outnumbered the Muslims and took away their land, he said.

He described AFP atrocities against Islam. He claimed there was a radar station on a high hill on the Zamboanga Peninsula, accessible only by helicopter, where AFP officers held Muslim women captive for their personal pleasure. (I couldn't help wondering how this, if it was true, differed from Reina's present condition with Janjalani.)

All of this, said Solaiman, was the justification for jihad.

Martin said, "Well, I guess Christianity is a little different. Jesus told us not only to love our neighbors but also our enemies. 'Bless those who curse you, and pray for those who despitefully use you [Luke 6:28, NKJV].'"

A big sneer came across Solaiman's face. "Where's the justice in that?!"

Muslims fully accept the fact of sin and believe everybody is going to be judged. We had already agreed on that general concept. So I said, "I, for one, don't want justice, because I am a sinner. I believe Jesus is God and came to earth to die for my sins. I don't have to pay for my sin, because it is already paid for."

He looked at me and said, "I don't want *anybody* paying for my sin. I'll do my own paying."

Later on, Martin reflected on this remark and said to me, "You know, that's exactly what Solaiman is going to do. Someday when he stands before God, he's going to pay for his own sin, and it's not going to be pretty."

We had already been praying for our captors every day, but now we felt an even greater concern to pray for their salvation—that somehow the offer of God's grace would break through.

In this connection, it was interesting to hear Allah described as Most Merciful—"more merciful than there are bubbles in the ocean," Solaiman said. Yet Muslims weren't expected to imitate this quality. To them, a merciful person was a weak person. Allah could be merciful if he wanted, but his followers had to be tough warriors in search of justice.

Martin said at one point, "You know, Solaiman, I hope my children don't take up the same attitude you have. I hope my kids back in the States don't ever go get a gun and shoot some Muslim because of what you have done to us."

A look of shock crossed Solaiman's face. "Done to you? What's my sin against you? I've never done anything to you!"

Martin looked at me incredulously, as if to ask, *Can this guy really not see? He's taken us at gunpoint from our families, forced us through the jungle, starved us, subjected us to gun battles—and he thinks his record is clean?*

We talked with Solaiman about the Koran and how only two of our Abu Sayyaf captors seemed to have read it completely through, even though it is only a couple hundred pages long, shorter than the New Testament.

"If I were betting my eternal destiny on the teachings of the Koran, I'd sure want to know what it said," I told him.

"Eternal destiny? Okay, let me explain for you how Judgment Day is going to be conducted." Solaiman then proceeded to tell us that everyone will stand facing in one direction, like Muslims do when they start their prayers. Everyone who has ever been born in the entire universe will stand, *totally naked, for forty thousand years,* waiting for Allah to pronounce his judgment of whether they go to paradise or hell.

People will understandably get impatient during this long wait. They will start going to the various prophets. First, to Adam they'll say, "Please go to Allah and tell him to judge us. We can't stand it anymore."

But Adam will reply, "I'm not worthy."

Then they will go to Abraham. He will say that he isn't worthy, either.

They will go to David, Solomon, and even Jesus. "Please ask Allah to hurry up and judge us now; we can't stand it anymore." Jesus, like the others, will say, "I'm not worthy."

So finally they will go to Muhammad, the final prophet.

Success at last! Muhammad will intercede with Allah, who will judge humanity, consigning those with good deeds to paradise and condemning those who fall short to hell—unless they were fallen *mujahideen,* those who had died in holy war and were thus already rewarded.

With this way of thinking, clearly the odds of reaching paradise were slim to none. The Abu Sayyaf didn't mince words when speaking of those who had "fallen short," those who didn't see eye to eye with the Abu Sayyaf and were therefore "not really true Muslims." This included even such notables as Muammar Qadhafi of Libya and the Saudi royal family. In fact, Saudi Arabia was especially scorned for being soft on Muslim principles, as evidenced by allowing the infidel troops of the United States and other Western nations to use Saudi military bases.

It was tough to argue with such logic. Whether or not Solaiman's information was theologically correct, to him it was entirely reliable. Of course, when it came to personal holiness, the Abu Sayyaf had their foibles, too. On the one hand, they complained, "Why does Hollywood make all this junk, all this immorality and violence, and then send it around the world?" We tried to tell them that many Americans feel the same way and don't watch a lot of those movies.

But then, someone would say, "Hey, Martin, have you seen *Silence of the Lambs* [or another film of that stripe]?"

"No. That's way too gory, from what I hear."

"Oh, we loved that movie! It was great!" they would reply.

Nor would the Abu Sayyaf ever think of turning away from a tempting situation. Temptation, in their view, was something to be eradicated from the world by rules, not something to resist through personal discipline. That's why they wanted an Islamic state. In such a place, there would be no bad movies, prostitutes, stealing, or cheating, because the rules would be so stringent that people would be afraid to do anything wrong. All the women would be dressed in such a way as to eliminate seduction. Thus, nobody would sin, and society would be perfect. To put it in Fatima's memorable phrase, "If you remove the temptation, there will be no sin."

Martin tried to counter this view by replying, "Scripture tells us that everyone is tempted, but you have a choice about what to do with that temptation. God always works on the heart of a person. It's not outside temptations that make us sin; it's our sinful heart, and God wants to change that heart.

"Christianity isn't a big list of rules. We don't have a manual for fasting or almsgiving," he'd tell them. "These things instead are supposed to come from your heart. That's what salvation is: a change of heart, rather than a change of environment."

They were not persuaded.

Our porch was almost the only level, clean place in the camp, so when it was time for sundown prayers, this became the location of choice. If Martin and I were sitting out there talking, we'd have to move. It was always nice to be out in the fresh air, so sometimes we'd just stand at a distance rather than go inside.

Then as darkness fell, Omar began his Arabic and Koran lessons for the benefit of the new converts, Sheila and Ediborah. We had no electricity, of course. He'd bring an empty soy-sauce bottle filled with kerosene and a rolled rag as a wick. I called it "the bomb" because it seemed so dangerous to me.

Of course, we, being infidels, weren't allowed to touch a Koran or even get near it. If it was inside someone's backpack, we weren't allowed to step over it, because that would pollute it somehow. More than once I was reprimanded for that. I finally got the point: Watch out for backpacks, and step around them.

• • •

The month of August and the first half of September turned into a longer and longer stretch of hiding, waiting, getting noticed by outsiders and having to move up the river, then back down the river, then somewhere else again. Days turned into weeks, and the hopes we had placed on departing hostages who had promised to work for our release grew dim. We were stuck with our lot; nothing seemed to be happening; the daily grind and Martin's nightly confinement on the chain became a never-ending cycle.

One time, Martin became very sick with a high fever and nausea. His joints ached. *Could he have malaria?* I worried. We had no way to tell.

In the medical bag was an antibiotic called Augmentin—a name neither of us recognized. But Ediborah, being a nurse, said it was okay and might help him. Of course, her practice of medicine wasn't exactly what we Westerners were used to; we had once heard her tell another hostage to take "two ampicillin tablets."

When I asked her if he needed to take the pills for seven days, she responded, "Well, you're supposed to, but when people are poor and the supply is short, we just take a couple so we can start feeling better." That seemed to be common protocol for her.

Nevertheless, in this case, Martin took a five-day course of Augmentin—and did start to feel better.

Fe dipped into the medical bag for an entirely different reason. One day I saw her coating her lips with iodine as a substitute lipstick.

"Fe, are you trying to make yourself look good?" I asked.

"Yeah. I just feel so ugly here, you know? There's no way to make yourself look pretty."

"Oh, Fe, look what happened to Reina. Don't try to make yourself look prettier than you already are. You don't want to get *sabay-ae*d, do you?"

•   •   •

Whenever the order would come for us to pack up, a deathly silence would fall upon the camp. My heart would begin to pound, and all conversation would stop as we began jamming stuff into our packs. I often found myself shaking uncontrollably, so much that I could hardly pack my things.

If we finished and the leaders hadn't yet decided which way was safest to move, we would just sit, terrified that a barrage of bullets would come flying at us any second.

The Abu Sayyaf never really had "a plan," it seemed. They just made it up as they went along. Sometimes we would get up in the morning, be told to pack up for mobiling, walk half an hour—and then sit three or four hours while they discussed what to do next.

One night after we had been walking for hours, we stepped off the trail shortly before dawn into a grove of banana trees. They put down a tarp for Martin and me, because it had been raining. We collapsed onto the tarp. I didn't even take my boots off; I was so tired and my feet were all muddy and awful.

In my exhaustion, I looked at Martin and said, "What is going to become of us?" Hot tears were streaming down my face.

Martin's next words just amazed me. With complete composure, he said, "We are going to get out of here, and we are going to go home." I heard that sentence from his mouth on more than one occasion. Every time it calmed me down. On this night, Martin grabbed my hand and we prayed together. We prayed for the strength we needed to keep up with the group. We asked that the Lord would shed his mercy on us and that he'd touch someone's heart to pay ransom for us. And then we went to sleep.

The next night, we were mobiling through the jungle when we came upon a river. We had no other choice but to wade into the water and walk to the other side. At one point, the water was more than chest-deep. Once we reached the other side, we were totally soaked and freezing. I found myself falling more and more as I tried to keep pace with the group in the dark. I tripped on a rock and landed down on my knees and hands so hard that it rattled my teeth. I just stayed there for a minute, while the whole group waited for me to move.

Oh God, I prayed, tears streaming down my cheeks, *how much longer can this go on? Is there a certain line that they need to cross, a breaking point where you say I've suffered enough? Where is it? Have they crossed that line yet or is this just going to go on and on?*

I heard no answer and somehow got up on my feet again to keep walking. A little way down the trail, I realized that I no longer had my *malong.* I cried all the harder.

When we were back at the river several days later, I saw one of the men with my *malong;* he must have picked it up when I fell. Of course there was no way I was going to get it back. For weeks I went without one, until Joel found a new one somewhere and gave me his old one.

• • •

I was doing laundry in the river when Hurayra approached me.

"A new striking force has been commissioned, and I've been

named the leader," he told me. "I'll be leaving tomorrow and I may never come back. I was wondering if you would sing me a song as a parting gift."

He had been so kind (relatively speaking) to Martin and me. I wanted to please him, but I knew I couldn't. "No, no, I can't sing for you, Hurayra," I said. "I'll just cry."

But he kept pressing me. My mind was racing, *What do I sing? A hymn or something secular?* I asked if he had any favorites.

"No, it doesn't matter. You just pick something."

So I started to sing the old John Denver song:

Almost heaven, West Virginia,
Blue Ridge Mountains, Shenandoah River . . .
Country roads, take me home
To the place I belong . . .

I suddenly realized what I was singing, and that's when I lost it. I made it through the chorus and then just quit, weeping in my heart.

"Continue, continue!" Hurayra said.

"I'm sorry, Hurayra, I just can't."

He walked off then to his mission, and I didn't see him again for several weeks.

• • •

One evening not long after that, a young guard came to see Martin and me quite late. "Solaiman and Sabaya want to talk to you."

We followed the boy up a steep, slippery trail, finally arriving at a little house. Solaiman began the discussion.

"We want you to make an audiotape for the Muammar Qadhafi Foundation." This was the same organization that had put up (or at least passed along) $25 million the year before for the Sipadan hostages. This was a handy way for them to appear magnanimous and caring in the eyes of the world while simultaneously financing their Muslim brethren's jihad.

"There are several phrases we want you to use," he continued. "You should say that the Philippine government and the American government aren't doing anything for you. So even though the Foundation hates the U.S., maybe they would choose to help you personally, as individuals. And be sure to include the phrase 'We would be forever grateful.'"

We had been hoping and praying for some source of ransom money, but the strongman of Libya wasn't exactly who we had in mind. This certainly raised an interesting moral dilemma.

Of course, they weren't giving us a choice. This was an order: Make the recording.

Martin took his turn first. I noticed he conveniently forgot to say the American and Philippine governments were not doing anything for us. When he finished, Solaiman said he thought that it was okay.

Now it was my turn. He reminded me to include the comment about governments. Well, at that point, I more or less agreed with him; I didn't see any action being taken on our behalf. So I gave my little spiel, saying, "I know that our countries don't see eye to eye, but maybe that would not stop you from helping us personally." I told them how much our children needed us. Then I said that we would be eternally grateful if they would help.

August 21
Paul Jones first raises the topic of paying ransom in a phone call to Oreta Burnham. No conclusions reached.

August 25
Zach's football team wins its first game of the season; Mindy's soccer team loses its first game.

August 30
Jeff plays wide receiver for the Rose Hill Rockets freshman team as they win their opening game.

On the way back to our place, we walked hand in hand in the dark. "Do you think we've done anything wrong, asking Libya to ransom us?" I asked Martin.

"We did what they ordered us to do," he reasoned. "I've been told you are not held accountable for anything you're forced to say under duress. So I think it was okay."

Of course, when we got back, everyone wanted to know how it had gone. We gave a little review.

Ediborah then said, "You didn't mention the Filipino hostages, did you?"

No, we hadn't, we said. They had told us just to talk about ourselves.

"Well then, you know what is going to happen, don't you?" she continued. "You'll be ransomed out, and we'll be left here, and everyone will forget about us, because Filipinos don't matter. You are the ones the world cares about."

"No, no, Ediborah!" we protested. "We weren't trying to leave you out. We just followed their instructions!" Martin and I felt horrible.

Two days later, we were called back for another meeting. This time they had us write out pretty much the same thing we had said on tape. Martin wrote:

August 15, 2001

To the Muammar Qadhafi Foundation:
I am a citizen of the United States of America. For the past fifteen years I have been residing in the Philippines as a missionary with the New Tribes Mission.
On May 27, 2001, my wife, Gracia, and I were abducted from Palawan where we had gone to celebrate our wedding anniversary. For the past 2½ months we have been held by the Al-Harakatul Islamia on the island of Basilan. We are well, but we desire to return home. We remember that approximately

one year ago your foundation was instrumental in the release of the European hostages taken from Sipadan. We are requesting that you would consider helping us also. I realize that our two countries have not been on friendly terms in the past but I hope that this will not hinder you in helping us as individuals. As parents we would really like to be returned to our family. They and we would be eternally grateful for your help.

Thank you for your kind consideration of this request.

They put it in an envelope and said they would send it out with the next messenger. Maybe this would be the key to unlock our door of freedom.

13

SEPTEMBER 11

(Rest of September 2001)

MUHAMMAD HAD MADE it clear, our captors explained, that slave owners were to treat their slaves with respect and feed them well. This was part of the Muslim code of honor: "What we eat, you eat," they said.

"Muhammad even said that if we are eating corn grits [a less desirable food], our slaves should be eating rice [the preferred food]."

It sounded good. But as time went on and the budget supplies got low, we started hearing a new term: "personal." People would show up with extra goodies and, when questioned, would say, "Oh, this is 'personal.'"

Janjalani and Reina's hammock was strung fairly close to us, and I began noticing that whether there was food in the camp or not, they always seemed well-supplied. I would watch them enjoying their meal, and feelings of jealousy would swell up. By this time, hunger was a constant companion.

One time on the trail, we had stopped to rest, and Solaiman and Martin were having one of their substantive conversations. We had left our bags just a little ways back in the long grass. The next time I checked, I realized that some of the young Abu Sayyaf guys had gone through our stuff and helped themselves to a bag of little bite-sized candy bars we'd been given a few days earlier! I was incensed.

rtin and I had been so disciplined to ration those out, even
we wanted to scarf them all down at once. We split one early
in the day—just a bite, really—and then split another one at night.
And now they were all gone!

The next time I saw Reina, I unloaded on her. "These boys!
I thought the Abu Sayyaf didn't steal! Didn't Muhammad say if you
steal, you get your hand chopped off? If that were true, these guys
wouldn't have any hands left!"

She must have told Janjalani, because the next day those boys
were reassigned to a different group.

It helped that every once in a while, Joel brought some coffee or
something else he could spare from his group. I'd always say, "Oh,
Joel, don't bring us things! We feel so guilty because we never have
anything to share with you."

"I want to do it," he replied. "My group always tells me, 'You
can take this to the other hostages if you want.'" Apparently there
were still a few fragments of kindness in the camp.

I think it was the hunger that made me start to see myself the
way I really am. Instead of being happy that others had food, I was
jealous and covetous. Or to cite another example: Haija—the one
who had been especially cruel to us, the one who had beheaded
Guillermo—had lost his hammock in a battle and was now having to
sleep on the ground like us. I could tell his bones were hurting—and
I sort of relished the fact that he was experiencing hardship, too.

I realized that when everything is stripped away from you and
you have nothing, you find out what you really are down deep
inside. What I was starting to see was not pretty.

(Soon after that, Haija and Daud were chosen to go to Jolo Island
on a "secret mission" in connection with Sabaya's younger brother.
We found out later that it was some kind of an arms deal. Soldiers
spotted them there, and when they ordered the three to halt, Haija
opted to run rather than be captured. He was shot and killed on the
spot. The other two were taken into custody. I couldn't help wondering whether Martin's glasses were still in Haija's backpack.)

I felt even more conflicted about food one time when a fresh supply came into the camp, but the guys who had brought it were visibly upset. Someone asked what was the matter.

"Civilians—we killed civilians."

"How many?"

"Oh, eight or nine."

There wasn't time to continue talking; we quickly hit the trail again. Late that night when we finally stopped, Joel filled in the details. He was really good at keeping his ear to the ground and knowing what was going on.

Their initial plan, he said, had been to stop any jeepney and take whatever food was on it. Well, the next one to come by was loaded on top with sacks of rice for the AFP, but it also had a number of civilians inside. Sitting on top at the front was a *CAFGU*, a civilian who is deputized to help the Philippine troops. This kind of person gets a very small salary from the government and is supposed to maintain peace and order in a given territory.

The *CAFGU* was holding a gun. When the Abu Sayyaf stepped out from the woods to stop the jeepney, he raised his weapon. So the guys opened fire—not just at the *CAFGU* but the whole jeepney, mowing people down with their M16s. It turned into a massacre—men, women, children, everybody.

And when they finally took the weapon from the dead *CAFGU,* they found out it wasn't even loaded.

They then gathered close to twelve bags of rice—the ones that didn't have blood on them. They also carried off the passengers' purses and bags. In one they were excited to find a big can of milk. In another, which looked almost like a diaper bag, they pulled out a little girl's clothes, some panties, a washcloth, and a little towel. All of this was brought back to camp.

Martin and I sat there in shock that night when a captor brought us hot milk with sugar in it. We were so hungry we felt we needed to drink it—but our hearts ached. Martin prayed, "Lord, we don't know at what cost this food has come our way. We just pray that you would have mercy and give strength to the families of these people who have died." I sat there looking down into the cup and wondering if that little girl had survived—the girl whose milk we were holding now.

A few days later I found out that she had not. And to make matters worse, she had been the niece of one of the Abu Sayyaf raiders. He had helped gun down his own sister-in-law and niece.

When I learned this, I just gasped at the ruthlessness of it all. I asked Solaiman, "What did this guy think of that? Wasn't he devastated when he found out who he had killed?"

"No, that was just their destiny," he calmly replied. This was the standard explanation for any casualty, it seemed. No big deal. It was just to be accepted.

But if anyone else harmed a Muslim, they didn't dismiss it as the person's destiny at all; rather, it was an atrocity for which they vowed to seek justice. I thought to myself, *Isn't this a double standard?* But by now, I was learning to control my mouth a little better, so I didn't press the debate.

The gun skirmishes continued, sometimes briefly, other times at greater length. The random firing of artillery kept coming, terrorizing us all. At the end of one scary day, during the captors' evening prayers, my nerves were shot from the constant bombardment. Martin and I were sitting on the ground along a rocky trail, and I said something that may sound strange: "Martin, I just need to tell you good-bye officially . . . so when I get killed or you get killed, I'm not going to have any regrets."

He understandably looked up in surprise. What in the world was I saying?

"I'm serious, sweetie. We have had a wonderful life together. I've totally enjoyed being married to you. We've gotten along so well; our goals have been the same; we both love the Lord with all our hearts. I have never for one second regretted marrying you."

I went on to tell him he had such a wonderful sense of humor. I said although I couldn't claim God had called me personally to be a missionary, he had called me to be Martin's wife, and that was enough to make me happy.

Finally, he responded, "Honey, this is weird. I'm not sure it's even real healthy for you to be saying this."

"Well, it makes me feel better," I replied. "I hope we get out of this alive, but if we don't, I don't want to have missed the chance to say good-bye to you and tell you how much you've meant to me."

We longed to embrace each other for a tender moment as husband and wife. But with the Abu Sayyaf no more than ten feet away, we had to settle for just looking deeply into each other's eyes. And with that, we got back to the business of setting up for another night of sleeping under the stars.

• • •

Somewhere during this time, word arrived that ransom had been paid for Angie and Fe. "But we're not going to release you quite yet," Sabaya told them. Why not? His response didn't really make sense.

As soon as he walked away, the two girls justifiably showed their anger. After all, they had been living for this day. Now the money had been paid, and the Abu Sayyaf was reneging on the deal.

I finally said to them, "Just pretend he never said that to you. For one thing, he lies all the time and tells us to lie all the time. This could be just a little joke of his. You'll be better off not to worry about it."

At about the same time, we learned that Reina had finally succumbed to Janjalani's pressure and agreed to marry him, as opposed to being just his mistress. She had been told, "If we get married, then you aren't Abu Sayyaf property anymore; you're mine. I can release you whenever I get ready."

So a little ceremony had been convened, with either Musab or Fatima officiating. Martin and I were not invited.

Implicit in this, of course, was her becoming a Muslim. She

didn't overtly choose to renounce her Catholic faith, but it was explained to her that this was just part of the package, and she would now receive tutoring in how to pray properly and read the Koran.

Meanwhile, no word came back from the Qadhafi Foundation, and about this time we started hearing about a wealthy Manila physician named Doctora Rose. She had been instrumental two years before in freeing a group of teachers and schoolchildren whom the Abu Sayyaf had taken. Now she was negotiating for our release, they said. She was going to pay $3 million for all of the hostages, not just the Americans.

Of course, Martin and I started getting excited. Finally, someone was going to break the deadlock.

She would call Solaiman, or Solaiman would call her to ask how things were going. She said that it would take two weeks to get everything together, and then we would be released. She was going off to a Hong Kong bank to get the money and would be back in one week.

After seven days, Solaiman called; she wasn't back yet—something about her needing seven *working* days to get the money, and Saturday and Sunday didn't count. But be prepared and be safe, she said; the money is coming.

A couple of days later she reported, "Yes, I've got the money. You guys start heading for the coast. I'll turn this money over in Zamboanga, and you arrange for a speedboat. We'll tell you where to meet up."

Solaiman began trying to line up a speedboat, but they didn't have enough cash. We heard him talking to an old classmate, saying, "Bring us the boat, and I'll just give you an OPM. I'll pay you when I can." (Solaiman told us that OPM stands for "oh promise me," a Philippine term for an IOU.)

Sure enough, the boat driver we hadn't seen since landing on Basilan showed up again in camp. We started slowly moving toward the coast. Our hopes began to rise. Maybe we would be able to rejoin our kids for the start of school after all. . . .

. . .

And then on Wednesday morning, September 12 (Philippine time)
. . . Solaiman was sitting in his hammock, listening to the news
from Voice of America on his little radio. He often did that—either
VOA or the BBC.

He called Martin over to his hammock. The two of them sat
there, motionless, for a long, long time. I watched from a distance.
What is so engrossing on the radio? I wondered.

Finally, my curiosity got the best of me and I could stand it
no longer. I ventured over to Solaiman's hammock. By this time,
Zacarias had come around, too.

Martin motioned me close to him. "Something terrible has
happened in the United States," he said quietly. He then described
how two planes had hit the World Trade Center in New York, and
another had hit the Pentagon. Thousands were dead. The world
had been plunged into crisis.

Oh, no. How ghastly! Our hearts just sank.

Of course, the word spread rapidly through the camp. Guys
huddled in little groups, talking and laughing and congratulating
one another. Everybody was really happy that Muslims had done
something treacherous to the U.S.

Martin and I retreated to sit quietly under our little tree. We
had so many questions, so few answers. What would happen now?
How would our country respond? Were the numbers of casualties
exaggerated? Maybe it wasn't as awful as it sounded.

That night as we lay down on the ground to sleep, we quietly
sang "The Star-Spangled Banner" together and prayed for the victims so far away.

The next morning, of course, Martin was over listening to
the news again. At the end of the newscast, the VOA played our
national anthem. The guys asked Martin to repeat the words for
them, so they could know what the song said.

Martin got choked up as he began to recite, "Oh, say can

you see, by the dawn's early light . . ." Everyone listened carefully. When he got to "the land of the free and the home of the
brave," a sneer came across Solaiman's face, as if to say, *Ooooh,
you think you're so brave? America has a lot to learn.* He made
a snide remark along the lines of "We'll see how brave you are,"
or something like that.

The full impact of the horror could not reach us, of course,
living in the jungle with no CNN or newspapers. What was rivet-
ing the rest of the world twenty-four hours a day in living color, we
were catching only faintly as through a keyhole. Still, we knew it
was a serious turning point.

Up until this time, our situation had seemed to be local, not
global. Everyone had thought of us as just a couple of Americans
in the Philippines (of course, there are many) who happened to
be in the wrong place at the wrong time. Now, the geopolitical
lines were more clear. A worldwide showdown was brewing, and
Martin and I were clearly on the side of the enemy of Islam, in
their view.

A few days later, after the buzz in the camp had settled down,
we went to Solaiman. "This seems like a very selfish question for
us to raise," we said, "given all that people in other parts of the
world are going through right now. But we must ask: Has this attack
changed our situation in any way?"

"Not at all," he calmly replied. "We already have a deal with
Doctora Rose to exchange you guys for $3 million. Our word is our
word, and we will not change that."

So again, we waited in hope.

• • •

The following Wednesday would be Martin's forty-second birthday.
I asked God to please, please get me something I could turn into a
present for him—a candy bar, anything.

A few days before his birthday, some guys went out to get the budget and once again were spotted by soldiers. They ducked out of sight, but the soldiers fired a few rounds to scare them away. Right after that, the heavy artillery started up. We all went running down to the river and hid behind one of the banks while shells exploded on all sides.

We ended up mobiling to a place in the mountains where we had been before, spreading out our empty rice sacks to sleep. When I sat up the morning of Martin's birthday, out from under the rice sack crawled a little brown snake, heading for the woods! I sarcastically said to myself, *Oh, goody, we provided a warm place for him.* Then I told myself, *It's not worth worrying about. If I let my mind run wild, it WILL!* I pretended it didn't even matter. But I did wake Martin up and tell him that a snake had shared our sleeping space that night.

That morning our group had nothing to eat. We packed up to mobile again. As we were walking along, the Abu Sayyaf started saying, "Happy birthday, Martin!" Muslims don't believe in celebrating birthdays and are, in fact, quite proud of that. But they didn't mind saying happy birthday to Martin.

"How did you know it was my birthday?" he asked, perplexed.

"People have been calling in to Radyo Agong wishing you a happy birthday," they said. They even gave the names of Bob and Val Petro, our friends from Aritao.

At noon, the only thing to eat was salt from a bottle that was passed around the circle. We kept walking the whole day. As it got closer to evening, we stopped along a trail, and for some reason our group of captors didn't want us with them. So Janjalani and Solaiman had us moved to another group, which fortunately had some kind of soup. They shared with us, providing a little nourishment on Martin's birthday after all.

But I was disappointed that the day ended without anything I could give my husband as a present. I told him how badly I felt. He just smiled and said, "You can make it up to me when we get out!"

That evening I remember he had an interesting conversation with a captor named Ustedz Khayr. This man was one of the most embittered fighters, passionate about regaining the Muslim homeland. He said the Abu Sayyaf didn't want to have to do things like the recent massacre at the jeepney, "but the Christian world has just pushed us too far, and we're sick of it. When people are oppressed, you can't hold them back. It's just going to be this way until we are given what we want."

Martin kept his cool, as always, and gently probed for specifics. "Let's see—just what all is included in your homeland?"

"Tawi-Tawi, Sulu, Jolo, Basilan, southern Mindanao . . . ," he began naming off the islands in dispute.

"So, if you got these—if the government decided, for the sake of peace, to give them to you—would that be the end of your struggle?"

"Oh, no, no," came the quick reply. "That would be only the beginning. Then we would be obligated to take all of Mindanao; after all, it's a wealthy island.

"And then once we took Mindanao, we would take all of the Visayas [referring to the midsection of the Philippines, such islands as Cebu, Samar, Leyte, Negros, and Panay].

"Then when we were done with the Visayas, we would go next to Luzon.

"When all of the Philippines belonged to us, we'd move on to Thailand and other countries where there is such oppression. You see, Islam is for the whole world."

• • •

We pressed on toward the coast, following Doctora Rose's instruction. We walked day and night for several days, until my feet were totally raw. Every time we walked through a stream, water and sand leaked in through the holes in my blue boots. Before long it felt just like sandpaper rubbing the skin off my feet.

At every rest time, I rinsed out my boots and shook out my socks. But still, my feet began to look awful.

We walked through several Muslim villages that were totally deserted. Some of them were quite nice; they even had paved streets. But the civilians had fled, knowing that wherever the Abu Sayyaf came, bloodshed followed. In fact, this pattern became so established that the military had begun using it as a clue: abandoned villages meant the Abu Sayyaf must be nearby. The terrorist leaders had even resorted to bribery at times, sending messengers to say to the village leaders, "Please don't leave. We'll pay you to stay in your area, and we promise not to harm you. But please don't give the *sundalo* a signal that we're here."

About this time Reina announced that she was pregnant. She told Janjalani, "If you want this baby to be healthy, I've got to be getting better food than I'm getting here." That was enough to get her released.

We got to a place where the Abu Sayyaf had stayed before. We could tell by the trash left behind: old, sun-bleached candy wrappers, fire pits, general garbage. Solaiman was on the phone, as usual, and also getting text messages, which is a big thing in the Philippines.

"Hey, let me read this one to you," he said to us. "See if you think you can guess who it's from." He then read: " 'Do you think I could come and spend some time at your place? Everyone is terribly upset with me right now, and I really could use a friend.' "

I looked at Martin and had no idea. He didn't, either.

"We don't know," he said. "Who is it?"

Solaiman read the message again, and then gave the sender's name. "It's from Osama bin Laden."

Could it have been true? Was the al-Qaeda mastermind feeling the heat in these days right after September 11 and looking for an obscure refuge somewhere? (I later learned that this same text message had been sent as a joke to millions of cell-phone users in the aftermath of September 11, but at the time we had no way of knowing that.)

· · ·

That same day, we found out that Janjalani, Solaiman, Fatima, Bro—almost all the leaders—were leaving for "important business" on the outside.

I told Solaiman in tears, "You guys are going to leave us here and we'll have no leadership and no communication!"

"No, no, no—this is a good thing," he reasoned. "I'm going out to arrange for everything with Doctora Rose. The speedboat will come and get you. You'll be out of here in no time."

"Well," I said, "it's just really hard for me to stay in this camp of enemies. You are an enemy, but at least you have been an enemy we could connect with. You told us some of what was going on outside. Now you're leaving, and we're going to have nobody."

The look on his face said that he was completely amazed that I called him an enemy. In his mind, he was just a wonderful fellow.

Soon they trekked off on their "important business," which I thought was probably no more than finding a grocery store. They took two of the three sat-phones plus Janjalani's stash of money, which funded our food supply. We were left to the tender mercies of Musab, Omar, and Sabaya.

There was one silver lining, however. Janjalani gave us his hammock as he left. After three and a half months on the ground, we could finally be a little more comfortable at night—although two people trying to sleep in the same hammock is not exactly luxurious. We found out that fitting two sets of shoulders at the same end was next to impossible. So we had to put our heads at opposite ends in order to get any rest.

Only on extremely cold nights did I start out with my back against Martin's chest, just to help us both stop shivering. Then

before long, I needed to pivot the other way. A few nights I even
retreated back to the ground in order not to be so cramped.

We stayed a few days there on that hill right beside the water.
Looking across the valley, we could see a finger of ocean coming
in toward a river. Across on the other bluff, we noticed AFP troops
moving in and setting up. Meanwhile, all was now silent from
Doctora Rose.

Could it be that the military had been using her to lure us to
the coast so they could flush us out?

In fact, that is exactly what seemed to be the case. I personally
don't think there ever was any $3 million, or that she ever intended
to ransom us. The whole thing was a ploy to get us to a vulnerable
place where the army could move in.

14
WEDDING TIME
(October–Mid-November 2001)

It was about this time that my ever alert husband, being mechanically inclined, discovered that his handcuffs didn't stay shut anymore. Something had rusted through.

We didn't tell the Abu Sayyaf, obviously. We let them think they were locking him up securely every night. But in Martin's mind, he knew he was free.

"What would people think," he worried, "if they knew I could have escaped any time from here on, and I didn't? Would they think I'm a coward?"

I just smiled and said, "They would know you were staying with your wife until the opportunity presented itself for both of us. And they'd respect you for that."

Now in hindsight, I suppose there was one night when we maybe could have gotten away if we had really been on our toes. They put us in a farmer's little shelter on the very edge of the camp. Right beside us was a big hill that went straight down to the ocean.

Could we have slipped out in the middle of the night, gotten down the hill without being noticed, and somehow fled to a town or army camp? It's hard to say. Anyway, we were exhausted that night and went to bed as usual. We woke up the next morning and hadn't given it a thought.

We always asked the Lord, "If there is an opportunity and you want us to try to escape, please make it clear to both of us, and give us the courage to act." That time never came. We never sensed it was what we were supposed to do.

I do remember one conversation about the fact that I wasn't guarded nearly as closely as Martin. "Maybe I should just go off for a walk and not come back," I hypothesized. "You could follow me whenever you got the chance." I wasn't entirely serious about this, but it was something to mull over.

Not long after that, I stood up to go to the bathroom out in the woods. I ended up staying there for a while just to cry. It must have been half an hour before I returned.

Martin's face was as white as a sheet. "I thought you were gone!" he exclaimed under his breath. And then he confessed, "In fact, I believed it so much . . . that I ate your share of the rice!"

We broke up laughing. But in that moment, I saw how afraid for me he was, and how we both needed to be careful not to do anything foolhardy.

Meanwhile, the daily dangers continued. The AFP was clearly on to our scent. One day the firepower jumped to a whole new level, beyond automatic rifles and artillery shells. Helicopter gunships with big machine guns blazing out the sides swarmed over our heads. What an ominous sound they made as they swooped down. Every pass seemed like it would mean our last breath.

And as if that wasn't enough—a group of A-10 Warthog attack planes then came screaming across the sky dropping real bombs. How in the world we avoided getting hit I will never know. Out of this whole battle, the Abu Sayyaf suffered no deaths and only one injury.

It rained that night, and there were no trees to which we could

---

October 5
Abu Sayyaf defectors lead AFP troops to the remains of Guillermo Sobero.

---

rope our *toldas*. So we just dragged the plastic over us for a little protection. We awoke the next morning totally soaked.

We walked much of that day, then returned to the same place to sleep the next night. The following morning, we were walking down toward a riverbed when, all of a sudden at the front of the line, shouts rang out, followed by new gunfire. We all hit the ground. The Abu Sayyaf were not intimidated in the least; they plunged ahead to see what was up. Soon we heard a scream. In time we learned that they had encountered three men at the river and managed to behead one of them, a *CAFGU*. The other two had run away. Just another normal day of jihad, apparently.

Whenever there was going to be a battle, in fact, Musab took out a little piece of cloth to make a headdress. He wanted to be sure he looked like a warrior. No matter what we were doing or how much we were running, he'd take time to arrange his headdress so he'd look cool if he died.

We just kept going and came to a farm where a young boy was working. I couldn't help thinking he was about the age of Jeff, our son. We all rushed for the ripe bananas that lay on the ground—all except Martin, that is, who was roped to a guard. I stuffed about four or five bananas into my pocket.

Meanwhile, they tied this poor kid up with his hands around a tree. I could see he was absolutely petrified. A little bit later, one of the nicer guys ordered that he be loosed. But they couldn't afford to let him go, now that he knew who we were. So—we had ourselves a new hostage. I felt so sorry for him.

• • •

We walked all that night and the next day. Once when we sat down to rest, Sheila came and sat down beside me. This was a bit unusual; she normally sat with Ediborah, both of them being Muslim now.

"I have a really big problem," she began.

"What is it?"

"Omar is *sabaya*ing me." Her face dropped.

I said, "Sheila, you're already married! How can they do that to somebody who is already married?" My heart really sank, because if this came to pass, it meant that none of the rules applied.

"I don't know. But I have to move in with him tonight. I just don't know what to do about it."

"Sheila, I am so sorry," I said. "I suppose you have to do what they tell you to do. But if I can help you, I will."

• • •

A few nights later, as we were walking in absolute darkness, Martin and I were allowed to proceed without a guard for a change. I was hanging on to his shirt so I wouldn't get lost. The artillery kept getting closer and closer. I was praying out loud, "O God, save us. O Lord, keep us safe. Please keep us safe. Don't let bombs hit us. Lord, keep us safe. O God, help us," over and over. I know Jesus talked about not needing to babble on and on, repeating yourself in prayer. But I couldn't help it. I was just too strung out.

On another night we walked until three-thirty in the morning. Totally exhausted, we lay down in a field. All of a sudden there was a big thump, like an artillery shell, but close. Suddenly the sky lit up with a bright light, and then a parachute opened up as a light floated to the ground right near us. Anyone watching could have seen our whole group.

"Oh, no, they found us!" Martin said, leaning toward me. "They're just confirming that we are here."

But we were so tired that we just lay there. Early the next morning, we heard the rumble of what are called "6 by 6s"—huge trucks with flatbeds on the back. These were full of soldiers. We got up and began moving out of this sheltered area toward a big field in a valley. Within minutes we heard somebody yell, "There they are! Hoy! It's Abu Sayyaf!" The guns started blasting.

Well, this is it, I thought as we ran and dropped, ran and dropped. Assad, the guard assigned to us, was handcuffed to Martin. They began running straight for a tree—and I saw what was going to happen, like it was in slow motion. Sure enough, Assad headed for one side of the tree and Martin the other.

"Stop!" I yelled. Just then they hit that tree. Both of them went flying.

Assad's side of the handcuffs (the rusted side) came off, of course, but still left a huge gash on his wrist. Martin badly wrenched his shoulder. They both just lay there for a minute.

Sabaya came running up and said, "What! What! Are you trying to escape?" He began chewing Martin out right in the middle of the battle.

Martin answered, "Sabaya, calm down. We are with you. We are not trying to go anywhere. We just had an accident. We are with you. We are with you. Don't worry about us."

They quickly put the handcuffs back on, still not realizing that they were rusted. Martin shot me a look, and I breathed a quick prayer of thanks to God. Soon we resumed running, as bullets kept whizzing past our heads. We eventually got into some woods. Along the way I lost my black *terong,* which had always been so hot and oppressive. I thought, *Yes! Finally I can start wearing something else on my head.* I really hated that thing.

Once again, the AFP didn't actually pursue us. We walked less than an hour and stopped to set up camp. By now the exhaustion and fear were nearly more than I could take. I sat just bawling my eyes out along the trail, with my legs pulled up and my arms around my knees, sobbing.

Angie came up to me and blithely said, "Gracia, what's wrong?"

How can she ask that after we've just been through a horrible battle? I thought to myself. At that moment, I'm afraid *Gracia* didn't respond very *graciously.* I looked at her and said in a snippy tone, "Nothing's wrong, Angie. Everything is fine. It is just such a beautiful day. There's nothing to worry about, no reason to cry." Angie looked surprised, then sat down quietly beside me.

The next day, Martin was asked to write a letter to an AFP colonel that would be read over Radyo Agong. It said, in essence, "Please negotiate for us, because even if you kill some of these Abu Sayyaf in battle, you are not going to kill them all. With God as my witness—and I have been a witness here during this whole thing from our capture last May until now in October—only nine have died. It is not the big numbers that you are publishing."

We had heard on the radio that the AFP claimed to have killed twenty-three Abu Sayyaf back when they called in the A-10s to bomb us. That made no sense from our vantage point; there weren't more than ten or twelve Abu Sayyaf to target in that particular place and only one of those was hit. What really happened, I heard, is that the AFP ended up bombing their own people on the ground, so that there very well may have been twenty-three casualties, but twenty-two were caused by friendly fire.

"Even if you do kill off all these Abu Sayyaf around us," Martin concluded, "there are lots more, and they cycle in and out. They go on a break, and then they return. So we must get down to negotiations in order to solve this problem."

• • •

Soon after that, the three remaining Filipino women in our hostage group had their own crisis to face. It was announced that all three would be *sabaya*ed.

Musab had chosen Ediborah.

Moghira, a leader in charge of the "blocking group" that brought up the rear whenever we mobiled, had chosen Fe.

October 10
The outside world gets its first photo of Martin and Gracia. They sit beside a smiling Sabaya who flashes a *V* for victory.

And Sabaya had chosen Angie.

All three of these men were already married, of course. Musab had two wives and Sabaya had three, although he had recently divorced one of them. But that didn't seem to limit the men's appetites for current companionship.

The girls were all so upset. Angie's and Fe's ransoms had already been paid. Ediborah, meanwhile, was a married woman (as Sheila was). What a horrible thing this was for them. We had prayed and begged God not to let this happen. Yet here it was. I could not understand God's way in this. I was just sick.

When the time came to move, Fe sat holding on to me and saying, "I'm just not going to go. I'm going to stay here with you."

"Yes, Fe, you can do that," I replied.

Soon one of the guys came and told her to move over to Moghira's place.

"No, I'm not going to go."

The guy took the message back, then returned to say, "Well, he just wants to talk to you."

So she went. She begged Moghira, "Let me stay with the Burnhams tonight up in the house—please, please!"

Soon she was back all excited. "He said I can stay with you! I don't have to go with him."

But in a few minutes, the messenger was back. "He wants to talk to you again."

Fe never returned to us that night.

When you are in a hostage situation, you just do what you have to do. You put the emotions of it all in the back of your mind and don't let yourself get carried away with how you are doing or how you are feeling. Otherwise, you would go crazy.

Since I have been back in America, people have often asked me, "What were you feeling at this time or on that occasion?" To be quite honest, I can't remember. My defense mechanisms had risen up to block the feelings. I was disciplining myself *not* to put feelings into words. My job was rather to put one foot in front of the other, to stay alive one more day. We just kept going and praying that we could get back to our children. That's all.

• • •

By this time, everyone was miserable from the cold. Musab and Ediborah had some extra plastic with which they would make a little windbreak.

I went to see Fe every day just to make sure she was doing okay. Bless her heart, she always had some food for me—perhaps a banana, or what they call *bianbons,* which are green bananas that have been roasted, then mushed up and put into a banana leaf, then roasted again. They were really good. She was always happy to see me coming, and we enjoyed talking together.

One night she brought us a big Tupperware cup of hot soup made of sweet coconut milk with little flour balls (like dumplings) in it. The mixture also included corn, some kind of dried beans, and I think some bananas. It was really, really good—what a wonderful gift. We enjoyed it so much that night.

Before she left, we prayed with her. The next day, she came back to tell me something, although I could see that she was reluctant. Finally, she got it out.

"You know that soup I brought you last night?"

I nodded.

"Uh, that was from my wedding feast. Moghira really wanted us to get married. I didn't want to, but . . . like he says, if I'm his wife, he has the say about what I do. He can release me, and it doesn't have to be a committee decision."

"Well, thank you for telling me," I replied. "If you felt you had to do this, we're behind you. You hang in there."

We prayed together then as we had before, but this was the last time. We didn't want Fe to put herself at risk with Moghira. As far as religion was concerned, Fe always told me, "I'm still a Christian.

Even though I do their praying and everything, I haven't converted to Islam in my heart."

The same scenario unfolded with Angie. She was quickly put to work as Sabaya's secretary, bringing us letters she had prepared for him so we could check the English. Some were about the Golden Harvest boys, wanting the local Muslim organization to send them on *hajj* (pilgrimage to Mecca) and also to college. All of the Golden Harvest boys had converted to Islam, or so they said.

Occasionally, one of the guys even tried to solicit Martin's interest. "Are you ready to convert to Islam?" they would bluntly ask.

Whenever I heard this, I started framing a dramatic rebuttal in my mind, something along the lines of *Christ is my only Lord and Savior, and I will never deny him no matter what you do to me!*

Martin was much more astute. The Abu Sayyaf already knew where his loyalty lay, and so he elected not to pick a fight. "Hmm, well, you know, my father is a Christian. His father before him was a Christian. Going even further back, my family has always been Christian. . . ."

At about this point, they would give in, saying, "Yes, I understand that you have a long heritage." And the subject would be dropped.

Sheila never married Omar. I'm not sure he ever asked her; I think he was afraid his other wife would be upset. Musab, however, started pressuring Ediborah to be his wife. But she held out for a while.

(Months later we learned that Solaiman, who was supposed to be out finishing arrangements with Doctora Rose for our release, had instead headed to Jolo Island and picked up two more wives in addition to the one he already had. The rest of the Abu Sayyaf were pretty upset about that. "He's off having fun while we keep suffering in the jungle," they complained.)

Whenever Martin mentioned how much he missed his children, Musab brushed him off with a comment about the hardship of being away from his own much larger brood. "It's harder for me," he said. "You miss your children three. I miss my children nine."

• • •

More battles, more running in the rain, more missed meals, more desperation. During those days, I began to notice the weight just falling off Martin, especially in his shoulders. I could see his shoulder blades sticking out. Never a big man to start with—he weighed 72 kilos (158 pounds) when we were captured—he was now turning into a scarecrow.

We stopped for the Muslim prayers one evening and then kept going. We came to the road and began walking along it in the darkness—something that always made me nervous, because it left us too exposed. But by this hour, we were all just kind of brain-dead, putting one foot in front of the other.

All of a sudden, right in front of us, shooting started. There were soldiers on the road. We ducked out of their sight. In the ensuing chaos, Joel was lucky enough to escape, which reduced the main hostage count down to six. Several of the Golden Harvest Plantation boys also got away, one of whom was carrying the medical bag. We were glad for them, of course, but also depressed that once again, we were still in captivity.

The loss of the medical bag meant that now we didn't have medicine or scissors—a serious loss for us all. A few days later, the one remaining sat-phone quit working; Sabaya's rather lame explanation was that "the thunder hit it." (Thunder?) Whatever the cause, we knew we were steadily losing our connections to the outside world.

My biggest physical problem at this point was with my feet, which had begun to ooze a clear pus. I put them out in the sun whenever we stopped. I tried to think of something else to make them heal.

In my backpack I had been carrying a bit of sunscreen. I was tempted to throw it away, because we really didn't need protection from the sun, what with all the clothing I was required to wear. Martin also had to keep his head covered. But I began reading the ingredients on the sunscreen bottle, and noticed aloe as well as vitamin E.

I told Martin, "Okay, maybe this will help my feet. It's going to sting like the dickens, but I'm going to try it anyway." I grimaced as I put it on, but it did seem to help.

Another thing that helped my mental outlook, if not my body, was remembering Scripture I had memorized long ago. I would have given anything to have had an actual Bible, of course. But that obviously was not going to happen.

One Sunday I found a piece of paper and began writing down all the promises of God that I could recall. My wording wasn't verbatim in every case, but I came up with quite a few:

> I will never leave thee / He careth for you / Will supply all your needs / I'll prepare a place for you / I'll come again / Honor parents & your days will be long / If we confess, he will cleanse & forgive / Ask & it shall be given to you / He that believeth in me, tho dead, shall live / Acknowledge Him & He'll direct your path / If any man open the door, I will come in & sup w/ him / I've loved you w/ everlasting love / When He appears, we'll be like Him / He'll perform a good work in you / I will not leave you comfortless, I will come to you / And lo, I am with you always / He that believeth in me shall not perish but have everlasting life / Delight in the Lord and He'll give you the desires of your heart.

What a comfort it was to review these eternal truths. In the face of the most dreadful circumstances, these were the words of the One I could depend upon.

A couple of days later, when I was in a slightly less spiritual mood, I thought of another divine promise to add to my list!

> Vengeance is God's. He'll repay.

Early on Monday morning, October 15, Sabaya came over to tell Martin to get ready to do a live radio interview. Although the sat-phone had gone dead, we did still have one cell phone that could be used if we could find a transmission tower close by. In addition to giving a prepared speech, Martin would respond to questions from the outside. Of course, Sabaya outlined five complaints against the West that he wanted made, which Martin duly jotted down on a banana leaf, since nobody seemed to have any paper that day.

1. United States support of Israel against the Palestinians
2. Oppression of Muslims everywhere
3. World sanctions against Iraq and Libya
4. Continued presence of Western troops in Saudi Arabia
5. Support for the Philippine government's goals in Muslim Mindanao

Soon the phone connection was made and the discussion began. When asked how he was faring, Martin said, "Well, I'm very tired and weak, and frightened. My wife is very tired and weak. We've both lost a lot of weight from walking a lot."

In a few minutes, the interviewer asked what message the Abu Sayyaf had for government officials, both in the Philippines and the United States, since the broadcast was being widely heard. Martin duly went through the list, as instructed.

But before the interview ended, he managed to get in some personal notes: "We would like to wish our daughter, Mindy, a happy birthday. She has her birthday in two days on October 17. So, this is our first opportunity to send them news that we are alive."

He also got a chance to address the AFP's rescue attempts: "Please stop. . . . Our lives are often in danger. Unlike the local hostages, it's impossible for me to escape. . . . I'm always tied up. I am always in the center of the group—not like the locals who are often sent to get water or sent to do small errands. The repeated rescue attempts and especially the artillery and the air strikes have been very frightening because they're so random. They cannot rescue me with an artillery attempt, and they cannot rescue me with an air strike. We will only be killed, and our children will only be orphans."

At the end, he summarized: "The Abu Sayyaf is going to survive this operation, but the hostages will not. Eventually, the hostages are going to succumb to sickness, and eventually some of the hostages are going to be killed." Thus, he conveyed that negotiation was the only sane answer.

Sabaya, meanwhile, took his turn on the air to keep up the bravado. He noted that President Arroyo would head to Washington the following month for a state visit. "It would be very embarrassing if she goes to the U.S. with the bodies of Martin and Gracia," he observed.

The only response to the interview in the days to come, as far as we could tell, was more pursuit by the AFP, more shelling, more raids. Things were not pretty. Everyone wanted this to be over, even the Abu Sayyaf. It had already dragged on much longer than anyone expected. With increasing frequency, guys in the Abu Sayyaf went AWOL. They headed to town for supplies and never returned.

The lack of leadership skills became more and more apparent. We ended up back in the general area where the jeepney massacre had taken place. Apparently, our leaders thought that the people, being loyal Muslims, would feed us and take care of us—forgetting that just about everybody in town had lost a son, a daughter, or a cousin in the shoot-out. These people were so angry with the Abu Sayyaf that they not only refused to help us but also went straight to the military asking for protection.

October 17
Mindy's twelfth-birthday parties are held at school and home. Her best present: a tape (from Radyo Agong) of Martin wishing her a happy birthday.

November 12
U.S. Representative Todd Tiahrt comes to Rose Hill to visit Martin's parents; he also stops at the middle school to address students.

The crazy part was, the AFP didn't believe them, because there had been no recent reports of sightings in that area. So one night, some of the villagers went outside with their own guns, shot into the air all around town, and then ran back to the military claiming that the Abu Sayyaf had attacked them. Obviously, we didn't hang around this village very long.

• • •

We began hearing that they wanted to release a good number of people—the rest of the Golden Harvest boys, the farm boy we had recently captured, and the Filipino women hostages. After all, Angie's and Fe's ransoms had already been paid, and the Abu Sayyaf were not hopeful of getting any money from the nurses' families back in Lamitan.

Sure enough, the rumors proved true. To mark the start of Ramadan, the Muslim holy month of fasting, on November 15, a major release was set up.

Oh, the emotional good-bye we had. I told Fe to call my parents and tell them I loved them. From my pocket I pulled out my wedding ring at last and pressed it into her hand. "When you get to Manila, give this to the New Tribes Mission office, okay? Tell them to send it to my daughter, Mindy, in case I don't get out. If you lose it, that's okay—don't worry. Just *don't* let the Abu Sayyaf get their hands on it!"

She promised she would. I gave her my dead watch as well.

November 14–16
Paul Burnham and Gracia's sister, Mary Jones, travel to Washington to lobby their representatives as well as the Philippine ambassador for more action. Two New Tribes Mission executives also attend.

November 16
Mindy prepares a Philippine meal for a school project. She takes pictures to send to her parents.
